Beyond
the Challenges

Michael L. Ham

Beyond the Challenges

A Book of Life Lessons

Michael L. Ham

All of the proceeds from this book will be donated to The Future Begins Today, a nonprofit organization which provides mentoring and scholarships for students in Troy, Ohio.

Beyond the Challenges: A Book of Life Lessons

Printed edition

©2019 Michael Ham. All rights reserved. First printing

For discounts on bulk purchases or to hire the author to speak to your school, staff, or organization, please contact Michael at: michaelham312@yahoo.com

Name(s) and identifying details have been changed to protect the identity of the individual(s) herein.

Editor: Loren Evilsizor
Cover and Interior Design: Kee Rash
Cover Photo Design: Loren Evilsizor
Cover and Back Photos: Amanda Brewer

Printed through Kindle Direct Publishing

For Scot Brewer, Gene Steinke, Chris Karnehm,
Brad Rohlfs, and Mark Evilsizor

Contents

Introduction xi

LESSON 1
Breaking the Mold 1

LESSON 2
Caring for One Another and Finding the Joy 19

LESSON 3
"Frothers:" One of Life's Greatest Blessings. 31

Photographs 67

LESSON 4
Embrace the Grind 81

LESSON 5
Accepting Your Mission 115

LESSON 6
The Definition of Family. 133

THE FINAL EXAM
A Return to Washington D.C. 151

Acknowledgements 159

Introduction

This book is probably unlike any other you have ever read or is in your personal library. This is because its author is rather unremarkable. I do not claim to have done anything famous or to possess a great degree of intelligence. The fact that you are reading this book has more to do with circumstance than anything else. My story, in comparison with some others, is not an extraordinary one. But the opportunities it has afforded and the people that have come into (and out of) it are extraordinary. I have lived a life that has required me to "grow up" rather quickly. It has been a process that is not for the faint of heart and one that no one could describe as easy. But in reality, who ever said this journey we call existence would be easy? The truth is that every challenge has been an opportunity to learn something and test the limits of my own strength.

One may well wonder at this point why I chose to write a book that is, for all intents and purposes, an autobiography. The answer is simple. I have had some unique challenges in my life. There is nothing in my early existence that would ever indicate that I would have achieved all I have. Being a nationally awarded public speaker, attaining a Bachelor of Arts degree, working for a municipality, and being the youngest and first disabled elected official in my hometown, is not exactly the resumé of someone born two months early with Cerebral palsy, raised by a single parent. Yet it happened because of a series of choices I made and because a select group of people looked beyond the obvious challenges I faced and saw the person in the wheelchair and the possibilities of what could be.

I hope this book will be of some use and inspiration to teachers and students. Teachers are some of the world's most courageous people, who make all other careers in our society possible. Likewise, students are amongst the most fortunate because good educators are not respecters of income status, family dynamics, or whatever other challenge they have to deal with. The most impactful and effective teachers are able to bring alive in their students their individual talents and passions. Next to my mother, the people who mean the most to me are either teachers or had some connection to my scholastic career. The pages that follow are much more than stories of the defining moments of my life; they are about making choices, overcoming obstacles, and finding the positive in situations that seem hopeless. Moreover, it is about the people who are closest to me and the lessons they have taught me, which have shown me a picture of the best of humankind. These are the lessons that I want to share with you. But in a wider sense, this book is for anyone who has had to embrace hardships in order to reach their goals. I want to introduce you to the people in my inner circle who have shaped who I am. From them I learned the qualities that are the hallmark of a truly successful person because every day they remind me that sometimes being good is good enough.

In telling the impact that these special people have had on my life, I want you to feel empowered to be a positive influence in the lives of others and emboldened to face the adversity in your own life. We all have the ability to do good for others and leave our corner of the world better than it was when we arrived in it. The obstacles we face, whether it is a disability, family difficulties, or other people's perceptions of us, all serve as stepping stones that allow us to learn and make us who we are. I hope this book isn't a real "page turner"; rather, you take time to think and reflect on each section and how the circumstances and advice within apply to your own life. I don't believe in sitting back and being battered by the challenges that life brings. I believe in making choices. Our choices determine the outcome of our circumstances. Each day, we have the opportunity to make choices. You will learn a lot about the choices I made, but what I hope you take away is what I learned from making them. In a world that teaches us to seek instant gratification and what is easy, my message at times may seem counterproductive. After all, let's face it, it's difficult to be positive in a society that inundates us with negativity and my philosophy is not easy to follow, even for me sometimes. But the truth is, what does not challenge us, does not change us, and if we are willing to make the right choices, good people and life changing opportunities will find us. All we need is the courage to seek them. In this book, I hope you find yourself. May it become a small glimmer of hope in your time of difficulty and may you be inspired to make a positive impact in the lives of others so that when people look at you they are reminded that there is still goodness in the world.

For the past nine years, I have been asked to speak to school districts throughout the state of Ohio sharing the story of the choices I made and the ones that others made on my behalf. I like to remind educators that the role they play in the development of young people will impact them for a lifetime. I enjoy challenging the students to look beyond their adversities and find their passion. I tell them my story and the lessons I've learned from the people who have shaped it. I want every young person I speak to or who reads this book to realize that everyone, no matter their state in life, all face trials, but in the end, they alone determine the direction of their future. I learned that lesson and many others very early on in my life. I want to share this and other lessons with you; they are ones we all know, but need reminding of, because in them, we find the virtues in life that are the most important.

Breaking the Mold

Life is made up of an infinity of choices. We make choices every day; they come in different sizes and can be as large as what college to attend or as small as what to wear in the morning. When we think of what it takes to be successful, that too involves choices. But how is it that we define success? Some may think success is determined by how much money is in one's bank account or the degree of influence they have over others. One of the first lessons I learned is that one measure of an individual's success is the way in which they respond to obstacles and challenges in order to break down other people's perceptions or stereotypes. When I speak to students, I sometimes tell them that I am as old as the Americans with Disabilities Act of 1990 – that's 29 years old if you are as horrible at math as I am! This groundbreaking piece of legislation gave all disabled Americans the right to work and live as independently as possible, outside the setting of an institution or care facility where many people with handicaps had been hidden away and all but forgotten. Now all citizens, regardless of ability, can be full and productive members of society. It was this shifting paradigm of the nation's thinking that I was born, on March 12, 1990.

I was born nine weeks prematurely, much to the surprise of my mother who was put on bed rest because of hemorrhaging in the days leading up to my delivery. The doctors at the time blamed her advanced age of 37 for the complications. At birth, I lacked oxygen and came out completely blue from the waist down. I spent the first two months of my life in a Neonatal Intensive Care Unit at a hospital in Central Florida where my parents lived. This time in the hospital enabled doctors to assure my mom that there were no lasting, harmful effects of the prematurity; although they concluded at the time that nothing conclusive could be determined until the age of two.   So began the waiting game to see what, if any, difficulties would come from my prematurity. Then at the age of two, as if on cue, the trouble started. As I entered the toddler phase, my mother noticed that I wasn't able to crawl or sit up on my own. She remembered what the specialists told her at the time of my birth about the critical second year of life and its possible implications for my future.

My mother was advised that she should take me to see a neurologist to assess what, if any, damage had been done to my brain. A quarter of a century later my mother could tell this story as if it had taken place the previous Wednesday. She recalled being summoned into a small examining room with me where the doctor took me from her arms, placed me on an examination table, and after a series of range of motion exercises, declared in a voice devoid of emotion, "Your child has Cerebral palsy.

He will never be able to walk." My mother recalled how she hadn't had the opportunity to sit down at this point and she described how her legs almost buckled under her, not so much because of the fear of the disability, but as she often said, "I didn't know what I didn't know and had no idea what to ask." It took me years to realize the defining decision my mother made and the immense courage it took for her to make it.

Like many other parents in equal circumstances, my mother knew nothing about disabilities or how to care for someone with one before that day in 1992. It would have been so convenient for her to become overwhelmed by the prospect of having someone depend on her to provide their most basic necessities for the rest of their lives, as well as the daunting task of enduring a lifetime of physical therapy, doctors' appointments, surgeries, and the bureaucracy that is the hallmark of living with a handicap. It is certainly challenging living with a physical impairment, but it is equally as difficult to be a caregiver because it is more than a full time job from which there are no vacations, sick days, or monetary compensation. As my mother tried to grasp just what it was she was signing on for, the good news was that brain scans and MRIs showed no evidence of any mental or cognitive disability.

This is when my mother made her choice. Her thought process was as long as I was able to learn and communicate, there was hope for a successful future despite the confines of the wheelchair. She made it her life's mission to not only be my full time caretaker, but more importantly, to teach me how to write and speak. She spent hours reading to me and devoted practically my entire second year of life to introducing me to basic number and letter recognition and even speaking in full sentences. I once asked her why it was so important that I learn to recognize letters and speak so early; she said that the brain is the most important muscle in the body and mine was going to have to compensate for what my legs couldn't do. In other words, I may not be able to walk, but I was going to be able to think and articulate my thoughts.

I give my mother all the credit and respect for her sacrifices, especially in those early years. One may wonder, though, where my father was during this formative time in my life. Reflecting on those early years living with both of my parents, it is interesting to think about the difference in viewpoints between these two people. While it is true that my mother was genuinely devastated by my diagnosis and admittedly grieved over what might have been, she knew instinctively when the pity party was over. I think this was one of the first lessons I ever learned: it is important to acknowledge our disappointment, anger, and sorrow when we face adversity, but there comes a point in the midst of difficulties when we must pick ourselves up, dust ourselves off, and move on to deal with our reality. This is what my mother understood. She had a faith and determination, which drove her conviction that while my situation was far from ideal, it was not impossible for me to use what abilities I have to be successful and make a difference. Conversely, my father, who always wanted a son and was elated at the time of my birth, changed his position almost overnight after the diagnosis. Instead of embracing the situation at hand, he was afraid of what he didn't understand. He often used to ask why this "thing" (as he called my disability) had to happen to him. My father had a perception of people with disabilities, which held that disabled people should be "placed" in institutions where they could receive special care. Being disabled, in his mind, precluded one from being what he called a full and productive member of society. His attitude was based on preconceived notions of "experts" definitions and characteristics of handicapped people. My father could never understand why it was that my mother wanted to devote herself to my care and education when "people like me should be put away" - to use his crude phrase. He thought that Mom was wasting her time on goals that would never come to pass.

Breaking down people's stereotypical ideas of disabled people is something that I have been doing most of my life, without even realizing it. My father may have had some very blatant prejudices toward people with physical challenges, but his viewpoint, however misguided, taught me something very important about people in general; society uses its perceptions of others and what we think they can do (or not do) to make judgments about others. Let's face it, we all do it. We rush to conclusions about people. How many times have we met someone and immediately decide whether or not we are going to like them? It's something we all do - first impressions are made and ruined within five minutes. Realizing this places a responsibility upon each one of us to present ourselves in a way that showcases our skills and abilities. The way in which we carry ourselves has a lot to do with the way people perceive us. My mother often used to tell me that by virtue of the fact that I sit in a wheelchair, people are going to look at me all my life - that is an inescapable fact, and they are going to make judgments about me right away. Understanding this, my mother said, required that

I make a conscious choice to show other people someone who is not defined by the things he could not do, but rather is someone made stronger by using his abilities to make a positive impact.

I was taught from a very early age that my ability to use my words would be the medium that would set me apart from other people in my similar situation. The first test of this theory came when it was time to start school. The district where I lived in Florida at the time mandated that all children with special needs begin preschool at the age of three. With that came the stipulation that all incoming students with disabilities undergo an assessment to determine their ability to learn. Thanks to my mother's efforts in exposing me to a wide variety of books and basic concepts, I was very well prepared for the tests that awaited me. If only the psychologists, intervention specialists, and special education instructors were as prepared for me as I was for them. The memory that stays with me of this experience is how amazed these people were that I was able to introduce and speak for myself, without a speech impediment. After the initial interviews, which appraised my knowledge of letters, numbers, colors, and most importantly speaking, I could see the shock on the faces of the three proctors as they tabulated the results of the tests. When they called my parents in to discuss the results, they shared their surprise. I had scored at a level that indicated that I could undertake a regular curriculum when I entered school, with minimal modifications.

Then came the small word that caused even my three-year-old self to pay close attention… "But." Because this particular school district had rarely, if ever, mainstreamed students with disabilities, they lacked the resources necessary to place me in a regular classroom. When I started school I was required to attend classes in a special unit for people with a myriad of learning and physical disabilities. These Multi-Handicapped (MH) classrooms, as they were called, were designed to teach the students, some of whom were unable to communicate at all, at a much slower pace from a curriculum that was heavily modified. As I matriculated through this self-contained and somewhat isolated system of education, the fact that it wasn't a good fit for me became more evident. My teachers in the earliest years of my scholastic career were always surprised at the speed and accuracy with which I completed my assignments and understood the lessons. It was often the case that I finished my schoolwork early or well ahead of the other students.

I continued in this restricted environment during what was a very unsettling time for me as a young boy. When an individual is not challenged or placed in a setting in which they are able to thrive, it can have an adverse effect on one's outlook. So I spent much of the time wondering what my future would hold or if I would ever be allowed to achieve something beyond other people's perceptions of what they thought I was capable of being.

During a routine Individual Education Plan (IEP) meeting in the second grade, my teacher made what can only be described as a casual comment to my mother about the fact that students in a Multi-Handicapped setting do not receive diplomas, but a Certificate of Completion. This was unacceptable to my mother, who made me believe, at a very young age, that going to college was not a choice, but a parental edict. My mother was dissatisfied with the fact that I was never challenged academically, but since mainstreaming had never been tried in my home district, she felt it best to wait to put me in a regular classroom, in the hopes that someday I could be part of the first group of fully mainstreamed, disabled students. However, faced with the fact that staying where I was meant I wasn't on track to receive a regular diploma, my mother snapped into action almost as if a cold glass of water had been thrown in her face. The next day, she requested a meeting with my teacher and the principal of the elementary school to find out what the process was for me to be mainstreamed into a regular classroom.

The short answer given to my mother was that there was no process for MH students to be mainstreamed into the regular classroom. It seems almost inconceivable almost a quarter century later to think that any educator or administrator could look at me, or any student like me, and think that I belonged in a setting that was below my skill set. It's important to understand that while I recognize that, I also believe that no decision that was made at that time with regard to my educational future was done so out of malice or ill will toward me as a person. Because if we are honest, we begin to understand that people in positions of influence make choices on the knowledge base that they have available to them at the time.

I think this is an important lesson for teachers and anyone whose job it is to have influence over the lives of young people. Teachers and anyone in the education field have a great responsibility and are called to one of the most noble professions in our society. Nevertheless, they also have to endure an endless amount of bureaucracy in the forms of standardized testing, state report card scores, and individual school district ratings. With the challenges that regulations such as these can bring, it is easy to understand why teachers and administrators can get burned out or even frustrated with their careers. This is made all the more understandable when considering the cutbacks in funding to public education by state and federal government, as well as, the amount of time dedicated teachers give to their students, which often has no correlation to what they are paid. However, as I have told hundreds of educators in many districts throughout my home state, what they do impacts their students for a lifetime and they must never forget that on the days when it seems they aren't making a difference. It is so easy to instruct students year after year and categorize them in textbook definitions of a jello mold of what we think they can do. But it takes real courage to stand up and look at each young person with their own set of abilities, which are unique to them.

Each semester my mother would request a meeting with the principal of my school, my teacher, and the staff of the Special Education Department with the purpose of convincing the powers that be that I needed to be included in regular classes "as soon as possible." Every time it was explained to my mother that nothing like this had been tried before. Mom would respond with, "There is a first time for everything." We thought we had everyone convinced to try it by the time I was in the second grade, so much so, that a teacher had agreed to have me in her class. However, just before the start of that school year, the plan was aborted because classes were overcrowded with almost 40 students to one teacher, and a seat could not be made available. I always found this rationale almost funny when considering that I would bring my own seat with me and it was even on wheels and could move! Finally, at the end of my third grade year, the school agreed to allow me to try to be in a regular classroom the following school year. I think this was done primarily in an effort to get my mom to shut up and put an end to these biannual get-togethers. But in truth, I had already been part of a pilot inclusion program where I was taking regular classes in the afternoon.

Mother got her way, with a caveat; I could take a regular curriculum the following school year, *but* and there's that word again, I would have to repeat the third grade in order to prove to the powers-that-be that I could, in fact, keep up with the other students and that this new placement into the mainstream was worth the risk they were taking on me. I briefly struggled with this ultimatum because I knew the connotations that existed when a student was "held back" a year. I wasn't thrilled with the idea of being a year older than everyone else in my class. Regardless, my mother pointed out that nothing worth having in this life ever comes easy and sometimes we all have to do things in life we don't want to do, in order that a greater good might be brought about in the end. Therefore, it was decided that for the sake of my future aspirations, being retained one year wasn't so bad. For as excited as both Mother and I were about what lay ahead, one person was very quick and unabashed in expressing his disapproval.

Living with my father wasn't easy. For someone I shared the same house with for twelve years, I don't have many memories of him and don't really remember any conversations I had with him that lasted longer than 15 minutes at a time. He had pretty much written me off as a problem that needed to be isolated. He was against the idea of mainstreaming me because he felt that anything good I ever did wasn't through my own merit, but rather because people took pity on a crippled person. He made no attempt to get to know me and I must confess that after a while, I gave up on trying to forge a relationship with him. Although we lived in the same house, we were virtual strangers. I soon learned that life is too short to spend it with people who don't think you are worth their time. Being around him was sort of like looking at a picture that hangs on the wall for a long period of time. It looks nice and appears at the right time, but mostly it doesn't do anything for the betterment of its surroundings.

Todd – I call him by his first name because he never allowed me to address him as "Dad"- was always around and sometimes even pleasant to me when Mom or a teacher was around. When no one was around, however, he would go back to status quo and ignore me. He thought my mother was filling my head with pipe dreams and unrealistic expectations when she would sit with me for hours on end at the kitchen table helping me with my homework, or practice my writing, (the specialists who tested me when I started school said that in all likelihood I would never be able to write) or perfect my elocution. Todd further resented the hours my mom would spend devoted to my personal care, or taking me to my ten hours of physical therapy each week, or to the multitudinous doctors' appointments of which I was the subject. Todd used to tell me that Mom was wasting her time because everyone knew I was just going to end up in an institution or nursing home anyway, a circumstance he tried to make a reality on two occasions. There had been eight years between the time of my parents' marriage and my birth. In that time my father got used to and enjoyed being the center of my mother's universe. Now he had to share the limelight with someone he considered inferior; it was too much for him to handle.

Todd exacted his frustrations on me in different ways. He seemed to be very jealous of me and my scholastic ability and whenever I got good grades on exams or my report cards he would always be there to say things like, "You didn't earn that, your Cerebral palsy did" or, "Remember the only way from up is down." The ironic aspect was he would never make any of these comments when others were around – those barbs were for my ears only. As harmful as messages like these are, I look at them as an opportunity to learn something very valuable; that is that the titles we assign people like "Father" or "Mother" are just that - titles. One must earn being called "Dad" or "Mom." Sometimes the people who truly deserve these distinctions aren't necessarily the people whose blood runs through your veins or whose DNA you share. My dealings with the man who was supposed to teach me how to be one have shown me that family isn't always defined by the group of people into which you are born.

A family is people who love and accept you for who you are: good, bad, and indifferent. But most importantly, they bring out the best in us and inspire us to give the best of ourselves to others. My own "father" once told me that no man would ever truly love me because the wheelchair I sit in impugns manhood itself. Not even I would fully realize how mistaken he would be. As I got a bit older and progressed as an Honor Roll student in regular classes, my mother couldn't contain her pride. She could see a future for the son into whom she dedicated so much of herself. Likewise, Todd was finding it difficult to hide his irritation about the fact that so much fuss and energy was being put into the first "cripple" to take regular classes in the Pinellas County School District. His often repeated question, "What's the point?" used to drive my mother to distraction. Still, there remained in her a small glimmer of hope that his attitude would change. My mother was the eternal optimist, always willing to give people the benefit of the doubt, always willing to see the good in everyone and all situations.

That hope was dashed by the time I entered junior high school. I was ten years old when Todd informed Mom, in a voice that was devoid of all emotion, that he no longer wanted to be responsible for a disabled person and that he greatly resented the time she was putting into my education. In his mind, I belonged in an institution, where I could receive special care, but more importantly, where I could be with others like me and out of his way. Todd insisted that unless Mother placed me in a facility (he just happened to have one picked out) he would leave her to raise me on her own. Few circumstances rattle me or cause me to fear, but I have to admit that this ultimatum did. Not so much for the fact that my father was threatening to abandon his wife and son, I never had a father anyway, my concern was for my mother, who up to this point, devoted her life to my care through being a stay at home mom. If he were to leave, how on earth would she be able to pay the bills and provide for us?

Had my mother been a lesser person than she was, she might very well have agreed to his request because raising a physically disabled person on one's own could never be described as easy. But apparently, such worries were not at the forefront of her mind because her reply was that in her estimation, he had to leave then because there would be no chance that she would ever consent to my being placed in an institution. He packed his bags, leaving Mom and I to face an unknown future. For as scared as I was for Mom, Todd's departure provided clarity in my own life. No longer did I have to worry about fitting into someone else's idea of what I should be. For the first few weeks after he left, I entered a period of intense peace and introspection trying to come to some kind of terms with my father's attitude and the fact that although we lived together for over a decade, we really didn't know each other. Being free from the constraints of his cynicism towards me enabled me to begin discovering who it was *I* wanted to be.

So often now when I speak to groups of young people they tell me they too have been abandoned by one parent or another. They share with me their anger or feelings of guilt as if somehow the fact that their parent wasn't the person they needed them to be is somehow their fault. I tell them that in the totality of a person's life the negative opinion or viewpoint of one person or a group of people should never define who we are. My father may have written me off very quickly, but in reality, that is just one person's perspective. Circumstances present us with choices and that which does not challenge us, does not change us. For a period of time after he left, I became very introspective trying to make some sense of why my own father disliked me so intensely and what I was supposed to glean from this man of whom I knew so little. I came to the conclusion that not only do we sometimes affix titles to people they are not prepared for, we also place expectations on them they are unwilling or incapable of meeting.

I do not mean that we shouldn't have the expectation that our family, especially our parents, will care for us and provide for our well-being. However, as sad as it is, the world we live in has taught us that just simply isn't the case for everyone. I have found that people are basically good, but because someone is supposed to care about you doesn't always mean they will. Coming to this realization made me appreciate the people that came into my life later all the more. I also found that sometimes the greatest gifts come in the midst of the worst adversity. In other words, in many cases, we have to go through our toughest trials so that something good can come from them. Knowing this certainly will never take the pain of trials and tribulations away, but if we are willing to look for the positive, we will find it, if we make the right choice.

Making choices is essential to overcoming obstacles and being the best version of ourselves. My mother used to tell me often that people were going to look at and make judgments about me by virtue of the fact that I sit in a wheelchair. Understanding this vested me with a responsibility to show everyone who sees or comes in contact with me that I am someone that should not be defined by my disability. This knowledge only made me stronger and solidified my choice to want to be of service to humanity. This is something every individual is called to do, to use our abilities for the good of others. The truth is that each one of us has a disability, it's simply a matter of degrees; some are more visible than others. The essence of a handicap or shortcoming is a challenge or trial we must overcome, and each of us can identify with some sort of adversity. Challenges are the one thing that all human beings share, that transcends class, race, and cultural distinctions.

Had Todd not held the attitude he does, he never would have left, and I would probably still be in Florida in a nursing home somewhere. While I performed very well academically, once I was mainstreamed, I blended into the crowd, so to speak, because there were so many students in such a large district that I felt as though I was a faceless number in a sea of many. It was in part because of this that when Todd left I suggested to my mother that we move to Ohio, where she was raised, to be closer to my grandfather. I appreciated what an undertaking being a single parent would be for my mother. She had already been providing for my personal needs my whole life, however, she would need to find employment and add an entirely new set of concerns to an ever growing list of worries. My mother, despite her best efforts to hold everything together, now joined the ranks of countless other single parents all across the nation and prepared herself for all the challenges and stressors that come with that position.

One aspect of life after Todd that always amazed me was that she never showed any signs of the unimaginable pressure that came with life as a single parent. After being a stay at home mom for over a decade, once we moved to Ohio she took a position as a job coach, supervising those with developmental disabilities placed in work programs. I'm sure there were times where she must have worried about how she was going to make ends meet. This is a constant struggle that many families in similar situations have to endure. It wasn't until years later that I found out that she raised me on $14,000 a year. Despite that, I never wanted for anything that truly mattered; my needs were always met. What is more, I learned to appreciate the things money can't buy. Traits like hard work and determination yield greater rewards than anything that is entitled to someone and while we should be grateful for what we have, we should never lose sight of the fact that the only thing that is truly ours is the strength of our integrity.

For as easy as my mother made being on her own look, both of us knew she was going to need as much support as she could get. As my mother already knew at this point, being a full time caregiver to someone with a physical disability is far from easy. Anyone who has been a caretaker knows it is one of the most important jobs one can have, but it is also one of the most thankless and exhausting jobs one can have, from which there is very little, if any, respite.

So moving to Ohio seemed a logical step. My grandfather, Lowell Bodenmiller, was a quiet man who had honor and dignity coursing through every fiber of his being. For one so reserved, when he spoke, every ear listened. As a retired fireman who served as a medic in the Second World War, he had a perfunctory wisdom that commanded respect. He shared my mother's vision that I would have a future, in spite of my physical challenges. So he was beyond thrilled when we, in fact, moved to Troy, Ohio, ten minutes south of where he lived. My grandfather knew of Todd's attitude and was more than a little angry with a man who abandoned his family when the chips were down. When we arrived in Ohio, my grandfather was concerned about the lasting effects that living with a virtually absent father would have on a 14-year-old boy. I remember him telling me that with new surroundings comes new beginnings, and with them, the opportunity to chart a new course. In order to be successful, my grandfather told me that I should surround myself with good people who would reflect the qualities to which I would aspire. Not even I would realize the importance of that critical advice or how much my grandfather's hopes would become a reality in the most amazing ways.

LESSON 2

Caring for One Another and Finding the Joy

The rain poured down in buckets on the August day in 2004, when my mother and grandfather drove me to Troy Junior High School to enroll me into school before the start of classes my eighth grade year. Several aspects of that day stay with me, the first being how different the school seemed from what I was used to in Florida. The size of the school itself was very different from the district I had come from, where there were huge schools that very easily made one feel overwhelmed. Here, I was not nervous about being overlooked and the staff I met seemed to genuinely care about young people and was very eager to get to know me and make sure I had the smoothest transition possible.

As my mother spoke with the Assistant Principal and completed the preliminary paperwork, from my position next to her, I could see a man standing inside the inner office. The bearded man looked to me to be in his late thirties, and although I found out later that I had overestimated his age by a decade, I didn't fully appreciate in that moment the impact this man would make on my life and how much of who I am would be due to his example. It was explained to my mother and I that Chris Karnehm had been tapped to be my assistant that school year, tasked with the responsibility of getting me ready for the school day, making sure I was at the right place at the right time, and in general overseeing my personal care during the day. My mother always kept an open mind in these situations because she understood that even with the best of intentions, she could not provide care for me twenty-four hours a day, seven days a week. She had to place her trust in others, but in light of recent events, that was hard for her. She was somewhat nervous when she met Chris, who with his wide smile and kind eyes, looked at her and said, "I got this." Later, Mom said that there was something in the genuineness of his words and the sincerity of his demeanor that allowed her anxieties to ebb and place her trust fully in Chris. I teased her years later saying that it was his Catholic upbringing and what she called his 'boyish good looks' that swayed her opinion in his favor. In truth, I was just as impressed with Chris as my mother. His openness and willingness to help others inspired me. But it went beyond that. To this day, Chris represents the best of humanity to me, not just because he wasn't taken aback by all the demands of being my caregiver, but also because he was the first mirror that I found. Meeting him made me remember my grandfather's recommendation to surround myself with people who reflected qualities to which I could aspire.

The values Chris taught me can't be measured in their importance. Each day that first year he and I were together, Chris was always there when I needed him. Not only to see to my personal needs, but to make sure that I had access to every opportunity to be successful. There is a common thread that the men who mean the most to me share: they are all very athletic and I, with the best intentions in the world, couldn't accurately differentiate an inning in baseball from a quarter in a football game. Even this minor point is one we can learn from. It is so important when dealing with other people that we be kind and open to everyone. The truth is that people do notice how we carry ourselves by the way we treat them and we never know who will end up being the most important people in our lives.

I'm sure that if at any point that first year someone would have told Chris that he would come to be one of the most valuable influences in my life, he might have turned and ran away. But that's not Chris' style. I learned so much from Chris and the way he took care of me. In thinking about that year, it is easy to think about the dedication he gave to my personal care and be really inspired because, as anyone who has been a caregiver knows, it is a difficult, thankless job from which there is little rest. My mother could have written her own book on just that idea alone. In truth, the impact Chris had on me goes far beyond being a caregiver. He showed me that each of us has a responsibility to care for one another. We can do this in very simple ways, a smile and a kind word can make all the difference to someone. Each one of us has some kind of challenge we are facing; the commonality that all adversities share is that they come to everyone and are no respecters of income or social status, age, family background, or ability level. All of us must understand that no matter the difficulties we face, there are always people who are in even worse situations than we are, and when we can, we have to do what we can to empower those we come in contact with, to live their best life, in spite of the challenges they face.

Chris spends every day of his life doing just that. During my eighth grade year, it would have been impossible for me to function without him because he saw to my basic needs and he also showed me what helping others truly meant. Chris possesses an innate humility which will not allow him to take credit for the impact he makes on the lives of others. He prefers to stand quietly in the background gently nudging people toward being the best possible version of themselves. My mother was like that also, her idea of hell was for someone to give her credit for anything, especially that which had to do with her devotion to me. She maintained that raising me and caring for me was her job and she didn't want any praise for doing what she felt was her duty. Parenting to her was very simple: you have to be willing to invest time into your child if you want them to be active and productive members of society.

I find it interesting that these two key figures in my life taught me one of life's most important lessons without realizing it. That is the importance of humility. People who make a difference in the lives of others and do good things never have to boast or talk about their goodness, and really shouldn't do so; one just has the feeling by simply being around them, that they are genuinely good. That's how I feel, even today, when I am with Chris. I tend to shy away from braggarts or people who have to tell others how great they are. As I tell each student group I present to, telling someone how talented or wonderful you are is the first sign you're not. People are smart and they will figure it out on their own. If you are kind to others, and treat them the way you would have them treat you, I promise it will show in your actions, without you ever saying a word.

Humility and kindness are essential to being a person of upstanding character. Using our skills and abilities to be a positive influence and encourage others is a responsibility we all share. Our lives are messages to the world about what we believe in. Each time we come in contact with other people we wear our character on our sleeves. They know instantly what kind of person we are just by the way we present ourselves. They can see whether or not we are positive people who radiate joy or allow our trials to make us cynical and jaded. Chris taught me the true meaning of joy and what it means to have fun. Life, by its nature, can be quite serious and sometimes just plain awful. Having a sense of humor and finding the good in every situation can help overcome any obstacle.

Chris showed me the value of never taking myself too seriously. He is always on hand to make me laugh and reminds me of the sheer joy that exists in laughter and having fun. We all have that one friend, who no matter what we do, is able to make us laugh. For me, Chris is that person. I started giving speeches in junior high school for various classes and organizations. Chris was always the first person to hear these talks. In those earliest speeches, I tried to impress audiences with my use of big words, facts, and figures. Chris would be very impressed with them. However, when we came to a word that Chris didn't understand, or thought the audience wouldn't either, he would always say, "That's messed up Mikey." Through this oft repeated phrase I was reminded that I shouldn't ever take myself too seriously and even practicing for a speech can be fun.

I remember the Christmas of my eighth grade year. Chris had been saying for practically the entire year that it would be nice if my wheelchair had a sidecar so that he could sit in it since he spent so much time at my side. So the day before Christmas break that year, Chris dressed up as Santa Claus and tied an office chair to the back of my wheelchair, put a reindeer antler hat on my head, and sat in the chair as I pulled him around the front lobby of Troy Junior High School. Later in the spring, Chris accompanied me on a class field trip to Wright State University in Dayton, Ohio. The university is connected by an underground tunnel system into which Chris and I got lost and separated from the group. We knew we were in trouble when we emerged from underground to find that we had stumbled on to the Air Force Base next to campus. Both Chris and I knew we were off the beaten path when we saw very imposing guards from the United States Air Force with more frequency. Once we got back to the group from Troy, one of teachers said we were lucky that we didn't get detained for questioning for trespassing on the base! These memories bring such joy to me. Not only because of their hilarity, but it also shows that if we are willing to be open to people and experiences, they will find us in the most unique and unexpected ways.

Chris did so much more for me beyond helping me find the humor in life. He also helped set me on a path which brought other people in my life who would define who I am now. One of these people is Gene Steinke, a seventh grade social studies teacher at the junior high. I had an extra free period during the day, which in an odd precursor of events to come, was usually the time when my cohort was taking Physical Education. Lacking an adaptive P.E. program, I was assigned to a study hall. Shortly thereafter, Chris introduced me to Mr. Steinke or "Steinke" as I would call him. His calm, laid back attitude appealed to me. When I met him, I was amazed at the interest he took in his students. Gene was relatively early in his teaching career in 2005 when I met him, and as such, he was free of the cynicism and burnout that befell many of the teachers I had come in contact with in Florida. Gene's only goal was to assist young people in reaching their full potential. Meeting Mr. Steinke was life changing for me. Here was someone else who could advise me and help mentor me; a fellow lover of history, just like me, who I think was impressed by this eighth grader's ability to articulate his thoughts in a way that was far more mature than the other students with whom he came into contact. When I met Mr. Steinke, we talked about the importance of history and my personal interests and a smile on loan from the Cheshire cat split his face.

I asked and was granted permission to use my study hall to serve as Mr. Steinke's student aide. He was one of the first teachers to allow a student aide into his classroom. What I thought no one knew at the time is that I would often sneak out of study hall during the first semester so that I could go listen to him teach. I found out years later that the principal knew full well what I was doing and decided that I should spend as much time as possible with Gene. I will always be grateful that the principal had the foresight to understand that in his way Gene was providing me the male role model which, up to that point in my life had been lacking. He is one of the most easy going and imaginative people I have ever known; his philosophy of education was to allow the student to become immersed in the subject matter and allow their creativity to shine through. Knowing that I had a propensity for public speaking, Gene would sometimes have me help him give a lesson. He and I would coordinate a frick and frack duo routine designed to introduce his students to whatever concept or period of history he was discussing. The fact that our personalities were similar made it easy for us play off of one another and be entertaining at the same time. Looking back, I realize that Gene was my first mentor. The first man (other than my grandfather) who I tried to model myself after. My year with him started my interest in public speaking. By allowing me to be his "co-teacher" of sorts, he showed me that the expert in anything was once a beginner, and being good at something doesn't require a plan, but a willingness to act. I had been giving speeches as school projects most of that entire year, but I wanted to get in a position to be able to give them in front of audiences. I discussed the possibility with Gene and his advice was simply to go for it. This is something that all young people need to hear, that their teachers believe in them and know they can do it, thereby giving them just that little push they need to really go for it!

Our culture is governed by words, and lofty ambitions, the most successful people, however, turn their aspiration into action. As you read this book today, can you think of some plan or goal that you always talked about, but never *actually* saw through?   The main factor which holds us back is fear. That is the most destructive force within the human psyche. It takes fortitude to be able to grapple with these feelings, put them into perspective, and dare to act. Putting me in situations where I could practice presenting in front of groups, Gene was propelling my thoughts into actuality. Sometimes in life we need something drastic to happen to help us change, that triggering event or person that snaps us into reality and calls us to action. As you will read, I've had several of those moments and Gene was one of these awakenings I needed in my life. We were the first teacher/student aide duo at Troy Junior High School, and through his faith in me, I found the courage to believe this would be the first of many speeches and unique opportunities that would come my way.

I'm convinced that the path to achievement is paved with people and opportunities who guide us along the way, but most of all it is a path laid by our tenacity and drive to never give up. My experiences have taught me that the world needs dummies. Now, I want to preface this by pointing out quite emphatically that I don't mean this as a put down or as a justification for not giving one's best effort in school, a job, or whatever endeavors we choose to pursue; quite the contrary. The kind of dummies we need are the ones who press on in spite of all the naysayers who come up with all sorts of intelligent reasons why our vision will never become a reality. This is the climate that I faced in the schools I attended in Florida and certainly from Todd. I know that many young people have overcome attitudes like this - perhaps you know one or *are one* yourself. What you must understand is that people, in general, respond to those who believe in them and challenge them to rise to the occasion of being the best they can be. That first year in Troy was pivotal because it charted a course which led to this book, and opened

the door to opportunities which I don't think would have
happened had I stayed in Florida or gone out to find the
people who could lead me where I wanted to go. One
such opportunity stands out in my mind.

Troy Schools used to require all the students in the
eighth grade to complete a job shadowing with someone
in a career path they intended to follow. As I did with most
things, I discussed my options with Chris and Gene. I
knew that I had always had a political bent to my thinking
so we talked about local government leaders in the area
and Chris had the idea that I should shadow the Mayor of
Troy. Thankfully the principal at Troy Junior High School
and our School Resource Officer had connections with
the Mayor's office and set everything up on my behalf.

My time with the Mayor taught me a lot about the
functions of local government, but also how that particular
form of government impacts the lives of people on a daily
basis. People spend a lot of time worried or frustrated over
decisions made at the Federal and even State levels; those
people and issues they deal with have very little impact on
us as the general public. But local government, our cities
and counties, provide services that impact us every day.
This was my first chance to see the inner workings of the
municipal government system and how it had the ability
to directly affect the lives of its citizens. More importantly,
that job shadowing opportunity showed me the power of
words and significance of using one's voice. Part of the
afternoon on that job shadowing day was spent attending
a dedication of the road on which the high school sits as
Veterans' Parkway. During the ceremony, the Mayor asked
me to say a few words. A request like that might very
well have overwhelmed another fifteen-year-old in equal

circumstances, but Chris and the teachers at Troy Junior High encouraged me to use my talent for public speaking as much as possible and I figured that an opportunity to address an audience of 150 civic leaders, military veterans, and citizens wasn't going to come every day, so I'd better make the most of it.

I don't remember the details of the speech I gave, primarily because it was off the cuff, with no preparation. I remember talking about patriotism and the importance of giving service to others. People applauded very kindly at the end and I thought that would be the beginning and end of my formal public speaking career. The following Monday at school, Chris being much smarter than I am (although he will never admit to it) contradicted my projection and said that I had tapped into a skill in which most people would definitely take note. I think he was more proud that I had given my first public address than he was that I had job shadowed the Mayor. He said that I had found a skill that would carry me far into the future.

My mother, Gene, Chris, and I were all thinking of the future as my time at Troy Junior High came to a close. For the first time in a long time, I looked forward to beginning the next phase of my education because I knew I was in a place where people would look at me as an individual and foster my gifts instead of just seeing a person in a wheelchair. Gene and Chris were the first people beyond my mother and grandfather to do that. Just as he did with Gene, and without realizing it, Chris was about to give me the greatest gift I had ever been given.

LESSON 3

"Frothers:" One of Life's Greatest Blessings

Shortly before the last day of school, Chris accompanied me to my freshman orientation at Troy High School. For many students, such a day lives in their memory for years to come. I am no different, although the reason may be. My freshman orientation of high school was not unlike the normal one. I was shown the layout of the school and given an idea of the coursework I would be undertaking. What made the experience extraordinary was meeting the man that I refer to as the "game changer", due to the pivotal role he would play in my own life. Have you ever had a teacher or a role model who seemed to understand life better than you did? Who took the time to get to know the real you and loved you anyway? Who knows your thoughts and you better than you know yourself?

For me, that person is a history teaching football coach named Scot Brewer. I had no idea then that this man would become (next to my mother) the most important person in my life. Chris and I had arrived for the orientation early and as we came down the hallway I saw a man who was around Chris' age coming toward us. Chris told me that Scot was one of his closest friends and that they were roommates in college. After Todd had left and we moved to Ohio, my mother said she prayed that a man would come into my life who could teach me how to be a good one. "I have tried the best I could to give you a sense of values and teach you integrity," she said. "But you need a man to show you how to be a good man yourself and erase all the negativity Todd left with you." I had my grandfather who was such a good example of all those attributes, but Mom wanted me to see that there were men out there, closer to my age, that were genuinely good people and would value me for me. Chris and Gene had started the trend, and they were about to put someone in my path who would not only continue it, but would make me, in large part, the person I am today.

Though I didn't realize it in that moment, the guy standing in front of me with the wide smile, would be the answer to my mother's prayer. I'll never forget the first thing the teacher, we as students called "Brew" ever said to me. "So you're Michael. I've heard a lot about you. I hear you have a big mouth." Chris had told him about my public speaking ability and I guess he must have been intrigued because I was struck by the fact that he, like Chris and Gene before him, chose to focus on me as an individual instead of someone with a disability.

As we toured Troy High School, Brew said that he was going to be working there the next school year as an Intervention Assistant and if I needed anything at all, I could come to him. My freshman year, in the fall of

2005, began with a bang, literally. I used to carry all of my school materials in a briefcase that sat on my lap tray between classes. One day, in the first few weeks of school, I was getting ready for class when I tried to place the briefcase on the desk next to me. What I neglected to do was turn off my wheelchair, so that the handle got caught on the joystick jerking me forward and desecrating everything in my path. As luck would have it, Brew's office was right across the hall. He ran in and pulled the bag off my tray. The punch line to this story, even when I tell it over a decade later, is that Brew saved my life that day.

In reality, Brew saved my life in another way that is far more important. The first thing I learned about Brew was that when he said something, he meant it. He told me that if I ever needed him, he would be there, and to this day, he still is here. I looked forward to the time I got to spend with him. In the first semester, I was required to take a Physical Education course. For someone in my position, this might seem counterproductive, but for me, a very unique door opened. On the days when the other students went outside, or played a sport that required some kind of agility, I would be permitted to go spend the period with Mr. Brewer in his tiny office, which I believe is now used as a storage closet in the high school.

That closet was where I began an intensive course of study that earned me what my mother called my B.S. (Bachelor of Scot) degree. For me, Brew became sort of a combination father figure and older brother, hence the term "frother." He has the incredible ability to fill whatever role I need him to take on in that moment. When I need advice or someone to remind me how stubborn I am, he's always there to pull me back and be the father figure I need to give me a dose of reality. He is also there to celebrate my achievements and listen to my concerns; he's there like an older brother who I can always count on for a laugh.   In one person, I saw everything I could ever hope to be. A model of genuine goodness who took every cruel opinion my "real" father thought about me and made it insignificant.   Todd always said that the only reason any man would care for me was out of pity. Just as Chris and Gene had done, Brew was about to prove how untrue that was.

Education is one of the most vitally important gifts that we can give our young people. Its value surpasses any knowledge that is gained from textbooks, lectures, or coursework. I believe that the success of an education system is built on the strength of relationships. Teachers hold positions of immeasurable significance and influence not because of *what* they teach, but how they are able to make each student they come in contact with feel valued and bring about their own individual skills and talents. This is the first lesson Brew ever taught me and it went largely unspoken. People may long forget the position or status we hold or even what we say, but what remains is the way we treat them, make them feel, and the importance we place on the relationship.

George Washington Carver once said that, "no learning can take place without understanding relationships". The one that I have with Brew is one that I treasure the most for the way that he took a fifteen-year-old boy without a father and taught him some of life's most important lessons. When I think of how my character and value system was formed, Brew's imprint left its indelible mark. Having him around at such a formative time in my life was crucial because the lessons he taught me were the driving force behind all my success in high school and beyond. I have had many wonderful, unique opportunities since meeting my "Frother" fourteen years ago and I'm grateful for them all, but none of what is contained in the forthcoming pages would have been possible without his example. As I think of everything he taught and gave to me it was almost as if he was giving me a blueprint for living.

It's common knowledge that no contractor in their right mind would even consider building anything without first having a blueprint or a guide as to how it should be constructed. In that same way, Brew, with his constant advice, encouragement, and life teachings, was giving me a blueprint from which to learn. I challenge every young person who reads this book to find the Scot Brewer in your life. If you have one, live your life in such a way that is a credit to the time and effort that has been put into you. For those who need a "Frother", be bold enough to go out and find one, but understand that once you do, you have a choice to make. Teachers and those who mentor or try to make a difference in the lives of young people can put all the opportunities and resources in the world at our disposal, but in the end, you and I are the stakeholders in our own personal success story.

Thankfully, being a stakeholder in my own life is something my mother instilled in me from an early age and I had Brew to help steer my future in the right direction. During those first visits during "P.E. class" in his closet, he spent a lot of time teaching me that we all have strengths and talents that are uniquely ours, and with them come a responsibility. I remember him telling me that I was going to go places with my mouth. He went on to pose this question to me. "How are you going to use your voice to help other people?" Something about the way he asked that question inspired me. It reminded me of what had initially struck me about Chris and Gene. They taught me so much about doing good for others; now here was someone challenging me to put my beliefs into action.

When one lives with a disability as obvious as mine, people around you expend a great deal of time and energy figuring out the best way to be of service to you, be it through caregiving, educational or professional support. Knowing this and benefiting from it made me believe so strongly in the fact that to whom much is given, much is expected. Now Brew was confirming it. He reminded me that as I had the ability to speak, I couldn't just sit back with it. I had to use it and be a voice for others, calling attention to important issues. Over a decade later, what is still intriguing to me is that for as encouraging as Brew was in bringing forth my abilities, he never once told me that I could do anything I wanted to do.

This may seem ironic, but if we think about it there is a lesson here for all of us. One of the primary roles that educators and adults have is to encourage young people to achieve greatness, in spite of life obstacles presented in their path. However, I think the way we go about it needs work. Don't misunderstand me, I get the rationale behind certain platitudes like, "There is nothing you can't do" or, "You can do or be anything you want." Such phrases are born out of a desire not to limit a child based on circumstance (and sometimes they are necessary), but if used to an excess, these clichés become an unrealistic easy way out. Take for example someone in my situation. All the best intentions and positive reinforcements in the world can't remove me from sitting in a wheelchair sixteen hours a day and turn me into a track star or an All-American athlete. So telling a student like me they can do anything, however well intentioned, is actually a disservice and easily avoidable.

I find myself tempted to fall back on those one-liners when I speak to students and teachers in various school districts across the country. I always catch myself and instead talk of how Brew went the extra mile to get to know me. It's convenient to simply tell kids they can do anything, but it takes real effort to look at each one as an individual and foster those talents that only they have. I tell young people to find those one or two strengths in which they excel and which bring good to the lives of others and do them well.

It was at the beginning of my sophomore year of high school that Brew was hired on as a teacher in the social studies department. I was beyond excited for him, not only because he was going to be teaching my favorite subject (I am a self-proclaimed history junkie), but also because now his "blueprint" for living was going to benefit countless students for years to come. He had already made such a remarkable impact on me and many of the young men on the football team, but now it was time to broaden his audience, and in a certain sense, mine too.

As luck would have it, Brew was in need of a student aide and thankfully he let me continue to be with him in his classroom. I spent every Study Hall period for the next three years with Brew and listened to every lecture and was on hand to help him when he needed it. Being Brew's student aide was a position in which I will always take the greatest pride. He made history come alive and is the quintessential teacher. What stays with me is how in the midst of every lecture he would take a few minutes to talk to his students about those life lessons which are the most important. Brew would constantly tell us things like, "never be afraid to do what you know is right, even though in the real world doing what is right may cost you relationships, status, or even your job; it will make you a stronger person, enable you to sleep better at night, and allow even greater opportunities to come your way". This is something young people, especially students, need to hear. Every day, they are tempted to do what is popular. Our kids face peer and societal pressure on every side, leaving them open to every sort of negativity and bad influence. Peer pressure, bullying, the decline of the family, social media and the society in which we live has forced our young people to learn some of the harshest realities that life has to offer much too early. In circumstances such as these, it's easy for anyone to become caught up in the status quo and follow the crowd.

This is where teachers can have an inestimable impact. So many students in school systems throughout this country lack positive role models in their environment. I was fortunate because I had my mother who gave me a solid foundation of morals and an understanding of right and wrong. But there are so many youngsters who aren't so lucky. That's why educators are so invaluable. Each year, they teach hundreds of students all of whom are fighting their own battle. Teachers have the sacred responsibility of educating young people, impacting the future for eternity, never knowing what they might do or say will inspire their students for a lifetime.

I have found that it isn't so much the facts and figures

that I remember from the course of my scholastic career, but rather the people who taught them and the way they made me feel. I think that is true in most aspects of life. It isn't our position or status in life that people will remember, but rather how we treat them. This is what teachers understand best of all. I once heard a TED Talk given by Rita Pierson, a motivational speaker and educator. It was called, "Every Kid Needs a Champion," and in it she discusses the value of a teacher's relationships with their students and the fact that their responsibility and influence doesn't end with the school day. Next to my mother, Brew is my biggest champion.

I became a man in the years that I sat in the back of Brew's room as his aide and in those moments I most treasured when it was just the two of us before or after school. I'll always be grateful to him for letting me hang around so much. I saw firsthand how he would take a personal interest in the lives of his students. I heard how he could always be counted on for a joke, an encouraging word, and when necessary, a shoulder to cry on. I saw how he would buy clothes and other essentials for students without the appropriate resources. In his role as a football coach, Brew was always proud of the success of the team, but always stressed to the players that the value of being people of good character, was far more important than wins and losses on the field. That message was carried through to the classroom also.

I was amazed at how Brew could take what would seem to be a minor point and turn it into a teachable moment about life in general. What is funny is that I heard him give every lecture for his classes three times before I graduated from Troy High School. I can close my eyes and still see him standing behind a red podium or pacing back and forth between rows of desks, flashing a laser pointer at his whiteboard to highlight significant points, trying to arouse deadhead students from their lethargies to inspire them to be actively engaged citizens who have a vested interest in their futures.   In his American History class, Brew would give a lecture about military strategies during the World Wars, using this particular lecture as an opportunity to share more of his wisdom.   He introduced us to the concept of a foxhole.

Foxholes are area positions commonly used in the military.   In the midst of the fiercest battles, soldiers would dig trench-like foxholes in the ground and use them as a defensive fighting position against the enemy. For the tactic to be successful, only the trusted were put in the foxhole because these were the people who would fight alongside you, die alongside you, and in some cases, give their life to save your life. Life presents its share of circumstances when we all need to build our own foxholes and surround ourselves with the people we trust and care about during those times which test our strength.   These are the types of people that make life easier to handle, those who will have our back no matter what. Those are the people we want with us in our foxhole.

Brew went on to say that this is a lesson from which everyone can learn.   Loyalty and dependability are two of the most valuable character traits we can pass onto the next generation.   He once posed this question to us, "Are we someone that others can count on?" This is a relatively simple question and one that I think, if asked, we would all answer "yes". Brew showed me that being loyal and dependable means a lot more than just sticking by your friends and those you care about. It has to do with realizing that a person's word is one of the few things in life that is truly their own. If we do what we say we're going to do and are people of integrity, that will show in how we treat those who are closest to us. Brew taught me that reality is the good you do for other people every day to enrich their lives. He also said it was important to love until your last heartbeat. When I first heard him say that I took it to mean that we should try to love everyone, and while that's certainly a very worthy trait to have, the older I get the more I think that the word "love" can be heavily overused.

People say it all the time, but how often do we really take the time to think about what the word "love" means? Each one of us have people in our lives that we love: family, friends, and mentors. We love them for what they do for us and the way they make us feel. Brew gave me an added idea of what love is. This is what underpins all the other characteristics. The idea that love, in its purest form, is the ability to put the wellbeing and the needs of others above our own and always being there for them in their times of difficulty. I think that is the type of person that everyone should have in their corner. Brew left the most important part of the lesson for the very end by telling us to, "be the person that everyone wants to have in their foxhole." Roughly translated, that was a challenge to all of us to be people of good character who reflect those qualities that others should see in themselves.

These "Brewisms," as I call them, have given me such courage in my life, but there is one that truly encapsulates the core message of every speech I've ever given and the way I have tried to live my life. That is, "There's no such thing as a free lunch, so when you get something good, don't keep it for yourself, give it back." Those words have been like a Post-It note stuck in my brain all these years. It struck a deep chord with me because he was giving voice to something I had long believed. I decided then that every speech would have the theme of giving back. I like to call it, *leaving your corner of the world better than it was when you arrived in it.* This concept is one of the greatest and most valuable gifts we can pass on to a new generation. Many school districts throughout the State of Ohio and the United States have instituted community service requirements in order to graduate high school. This is a great way to get students in the mindset of considering the needs of others. But it isn't enough to talk about it or mandate it without making sure that its value is understood. Young people learn by example. They have to see the people around them participating in events that positively improve the world around them. Rather we realize it or not, each one of us leaves a legacy everywhere we go; in one hundred years people will know that we were in the world by the indelible mark we have left. How will they know it? By the positive contributions we make to the betterment of others. A fundamental fact of life is that the truest test of our actions is how long the good in those actions last.

Are we putting that attitude into practice? Do we give back to our school or community? Brew challenged us as students to do one thing a day to make a person smile. As my local public speaking assignments became more prevalent, I was surrounded by professionals who were on several boards and committees, all of which served to play an essential role in making Troy a great place to live. Not everyone is going to be in a position where they can serve on a nonprofit board or give vast sums of money, and that's okay. Goodness and service to others shine through one small act at a time.

We all have a responsibility to instill in our youth the desire to give. This is a part of life which is so necessary, but it must be taught early. If we can teach our students to do little acts of kindness now, they will grow with an attitude of gratitude. Brew told me that, "character is the good we do for others every day, with no expectation of anything in return". That gave me courage to go out and use my speaking ability as a tool that would be a positive force to anyone that hears it.

I crafted the first award-winning speech of my high school career as a junior. I joined two organizations which had competitive public speaking. The first was the Family, Career, and Community Leaders of America (FCCLA) and the other was the Troy High School Speech and Debate Team. FCCLA, for whom this particular speech was written, touted itself as the largest student leadership organization in the country, thanks in part to its emphasis on community service. As I was preparing the presentation, I kept Brew's words in the forefront of my mind. Any speech for FCCLA had to tie in to one of their central themes of leadership or community service. So after talking it over with the advisor and Brew, I decided to speak about living with a disability and using our individual gifts to give back to others.

In the speech, I raised a point that I believe is vitally important to living life to the fullest. We all have some kind of disability, some, however, are more visible than others. The essence of the word *disability* is a challenge or shortcoming that we must work to overcome. It can be very easy to use these obstacles as excuses or crutches for why we aren't using the talents we have to reach our full potential. Like most things in life, avoiding this pitfall requires a decision. Imagine if at any point in my life I would have chosen to be overcome by my disability or the fact that my father chose to have nothing to do with me. I would have missed out on some wonderful opportunities, not to mention a relationship with a remarkable mentor and brother who has put up with me longer than my own father did, who showed me that true joy comes from keeping your mind and heart open to experiences and people that enrich the soul.

The presentation, entitled, "Diversity in American Legislation," discussed living with a disability, the laws that have made it possible for those *with* disabilities to be as productive as possible, and most importantly, the responsibility that all people have regardless of what challenges they face, handicap or otherwise, to use what talents we have been given to improve ourselves and the people around us. I contended then (and still do) that what happens to most people is that we talk ourselves out of using our strengths because we tend to allow the trials in our lives to be used as reasons why we aren't truly living. Everyone exists, but few people live and enjoy life by choosing to find the good. It's very easy to be pessimistic about the situations in which we may find ourselves. But being optimistic requires taking a look at ourselves, and realizing that while things may not be at their best or even ideal, there is always something in our lives that is cause for hope that we can do which will serve as an example to everyone around us of how to overcome adversity.

It was this message that I took to competition for FCCLA, and in the process of crafting it, I learned the way in which you prepare for a speech, or practice any talent you have is as valuable as the talent itself. Once I wrote the speech, the organization required that I present it to as many audiences as possible in order to become more comfortable delivering messages in front of groups. So I spoke to the Optimist Club, the Rotary Club, and whatever other organization needed a free stump speaker. While these opportunities gave me a platform to perfect my skills and speak about topics that need attention brought to them, the best part of preparing for a presentation was the one-on-one time I got with Brew.

I was in his room constantly before and after school preparing for speech competitions or seeking his counsel about one thing or another. He is a great captive audience, even now when I need to practice a speech. Brew's support was the lifeblood of the success behind my public speaking career, in the same way that athletes lift weights or listen to music before playing, I was with Brew before each speech competition having a conversation that we had so often it could have been scripted. I would roll in his classroom on the day before my speech and ask for a piece of advice that I could carry with me as I was presenting. Without exception, Brew's dictum was pretty much the same every time; he would use those moments to impart a formula of sorts that has remained unchanged to this day with every talk I give, no matter the subject.

Brew began by giving me a directive that one of his football coaches had given to him. "Be yourself", might sound like simple advice, however, it's one that is so vital to doing anything that is worthwhile. We are bombarded everyday with images and ideals of perfection and success that have become so much a part of culture that people have become great copycats. They feel as though they haven't truly "made it" unless they look and act like those they define as successful. Young people, especially, are quick to idolize celebrities and the peers around them who are popular. Role models are a wonderful gift, mine have shown me the value of individuality. This speaks again to the incredible power that teachers have. Good educators know that in spite of what state mandates and standardized testing might suggest, no two students learn in the same way or share the same life experiences, so they work to bring out those qualities in their students that define them as individuals.

Have you ever considered your fingerprint? There is not another one like yours in the entire world and there never will be. It is inconceivable then that we would try to duplicate anyone else when we are born to stand out. I mistakenly thought that in order to give a successful oration, one had to adopt the same speaking style as a Winston Churchill or a Ronald Reagan. But Brew told me that my messages have merit enough on their own without having to emulate anyone else. Because the talks, especially, "Diversity in American Legislation" had such important themes, he constantly encouraged me to speak from the heart. "If you can't say it from the heart", he contended, "shut up." I had the habit of constantly looking at my manuscript when I was speaking and forgetting to make eye contact with the audience (and Brew when practicing) and looking at the copy as if to read it. He was determined to break me of this monumental pitfall for public speakers, even placing his youngest newborn daughter Payton in my arms so that I was unable to hold my script. Without fail, Brew would stop me and tell me to look at him and believe in what I was saying enough that it comes from the heart and is sincere. For all the work that he did to make me into a public speaker, I think it's really Payton that deserves the credit. Had I not been so concerned about dropping the baby who would grow into my favorite young lady, I might not have won any awards for my public speaking!

We get out of life what we put into it. Drive and determination are the keys to being successful in anything, therefore, we should always strive to give one hundred percent to everything we do. I learned this from Brew as he was helping me prepare for speeches. To this day, I am astonished by the time that he gave to me. Despite the responsibilities that being a teacher, football coach, husband, brother, son, and new father presented, he always somehow managed to find the time to be there when I needed him. Even today, he still is and that has taught me a great lesson about time.

Giving to others requires sacrifice. It is easy to give possessions and money, but the hardest and most valuable commodity to part with is time, primarily because none of us seem to have enough of it. However, if we truly wish to make a difference, giving of our time is essential. Again, this is a very basic concept that everyone knows, but how often do we put that into practice? Do we take time to get to know people, not for what we perceive them to be, but for who they really are? When was the last time we took the time to walk in someone else's shoes and try to understand the struggles they have to endure? How long has it been since we called or made a visit to someone we love and told them how much we appreciate them being in our lives? Everyone should ask themselves these questions at some point.

Once I became an awarded public speaker, people often ask if there is a secret to giving an effective talk. I know I'm supposed to say that practice and effort are the essential makings of doing anything well and indeed that's true. But more than that, I think the time that Brew spent with me, when he could have been doing any number of other things, placed an added responsibility on me. It showed me that to be a good influence we have to spend time meeting people where they are, and it also made me want to do well for him as a thank you for the time he put into helping me. This is important for students to understand; the adults in their lives, whether they be parents, teachers, coaches, ministers, or others, dedicate their lives to making sure they have everything they need to be successful. Very seldom do teachers ever hear, "Thank You!" from the students they impact. This is part of what drove my achievement. I realized that whatever good I did, be it through academics, public speaking, or through small acts of kindness, those were a tribute to my mother, Chris, Gene, and especially Brew for molding me into the person I am today.

March of each year signaled a very busy, but nevertheless, exciting time for me at Troy High School. It was during that time when the FCCLA's competitive events began. I had already been giving speeches as a part of the Troy High School Speech and Debate Team, as that season went from November to February. After it was finished, it was time to begin drafting a presentation for FCCLA.

My junior year was no exception. As I was preparing for the regional competition, I somehow knew that this speech was going to be different. I had participated in the speech competition during my sophomore year and advanced to the state level with a speech about what it's like to live with a disability.

To be honest, I was a bit hesitant to talk about my own handicap because I never wanted it to look as though I was gaining sympathy or acclaim for what was, in essence, an accident of circumstance. Brew used my trepidation into a teachable moment. He said that, like it or not, my disability is part of who I am and no matter how annoying it may be at times, I can't ignore it, and, if presented correctly, this talk could be one that gives a voice to the voiceless and makes others understand how fortunate they are and that their ability to positively impact the world around them is independent of any challenge they face. That is how my speech, "Diversity in American Legislation" was crafted. Living with a person who is challenged with a disability was one facet of it, but I also brought in the idea of service above self and discussed how legislation has made it possible for people of all ability levels to live beyond their adversities. Brew is the only person I ever met who could give a person in a wheelchair the kick in the pants they needed to stray outside their comfort zone.

The risk paid off when I earned a perfect score at the regional competition. This meant that I qualified again to speak in Columbus at the FCCLA State Convention. This was a unique experience for me. I spent months preparing for an oration, giving it in front of countless audiences, all of which came down to a ten-minute presentation in front of three judges. I wasn't nervous by the day of the competition itself, nor am I for any talk I give. Brew's advice really rings true: if you speak from the heart and believe in what you say, others will listen.

This was the attitude I took when I went to one of the buildings on the Columbus Fairgrounds which had been partitioned so that several speeches could be given at one time without disruption. The talk was well received by the three judges that heard it, one of which was a Colonel in the Air Force who flew President Reagan in Marine One, the President's helicopter. They asked questions about my involvement at Troy High School and seemed to be impressed by the amount of public speaking I had done in front of various groups and organizations. After declaring the talk the best they had seen all day and wishing me good luck, there was nothing left to do, but wait with my mother and the Troy FCCLA advisor for the results to come in. For all the time and effort it takes to prepare and give a presentation, my mother contended that the waiting for competitive speaking scores is worse than having to listen to me give the speech one hundred times in rehearsal. If anyone had the right to be anxious, it was my mother. Her dedication enabled me to partake in all of these unique opportunities. She drove me to speaking engagements, made sure I looked presentable and professional, and saw to all the small details that allowed me to go out and give talks. Mom was also so grateful for Brew because here was a man who loved me just as much as she did and dedicated himself to helping me have the most successful future possible.

So many thoughts were coursing through my brain the next morning as I sat in a crowd of three thousand FCCLA advisors, parents, and students who were competing in various leadership oriented events like Parliamentary Procedure, Job Interviews, and my own, Illustrated Talk. More than anything, I wanted to be a credit to my mother, Brew, my FCCLA advisor and all the other teachers at Troy High School who had put their time and effort into making everything that I had done up to that point possible. As they were getting ready to announce gold medalists and those who qualified to compete at the 2008 FCCLA National Leadership Conference, I felt myself begin to get surprisingly nervous. The time came to announce medal winners in the Illustrated Talk event; I needed at least 90 out of 100 points to earn a medal.

My anticipation level rose all the higher as they announced the national qualifiers. Everyone who heard my talk said that it was unlike any other that would be featured at the competition so I thought I might have a chance to advance to the next stage. Sure enough, my name and the title of the speech were announced as moving on to the National Competition in Orlando, Florida that July! I was conducted to the stage to receive a trophy, which was presented only to those who qualified to advance to the national competition in Orlando. I couldn't help but think about how far I had come from the prospect of never receiving a high school diploma in Florida with a father who cast me aside, to finding positive male role models and using my voice to influence people in a positive way. As they handed me the trophy, which when placed on my wheelchair lap tray was taller than my line of sight, I couldn't wait to get back to Troy and share my euphoria with Brew. I knew he would be just as excited and proud as my mother and I were. This is the best part of having a "frother" in your corner; they stick by you through thick and thin and are just as enthusiastic about your accomplishments as their own.

The months after the state competition leading up to the end of my junior year brought with it more speaking opportunities to organizations within my community. Everyone I came in contact with seemed eager to hear about the first Troy student ever to participate in a national speech event. You would think that being the first to do anything is easy, after all, if you do it totally wrong, none is any the wiser. However, I found that it actually sets the bar for all those who will come after you. I can honestly say I had no idea what I was doing in those early public speeches. I just accepted invitations to speak to groups as they would come in. Just as I had done preparing for State, I spoke to any and all groups that sent invitations: schools, service clubs, and political groups allowed me to come and hone my oratory skills on their audiences. The Mayor of Troy and the former President of City Council, who had stayed in contact with me since my eighth grade job shadowing, procured speaking engagements for me and were on hand to give advice about the content and structure of the talks as the topics became more varied. I was astonished at the number of times people would give standing ovations and laud my speaking ability. Audiences were eager to hear more than just the speech that I was taking to a national competition; they were equally interested in the person behind it, and amazingly enough, how he was overcoming the challenges of being a disabled young man in a wheelchair.

Thankfully, I had Brew at my side every day at school, taking every breath of this experience with me. He was the one person who could build me up on those rare days when

I wasn't sure how a particular message would be received. I was the first student ever in the history of Troy Schools to speak competitively on a national level. Being the first to do anything places on you an awesome responsibility, because no matter what it is, the way you perform sets the bar for all those who will come after. More importantly, being the first teaches you to live in the present moment. As much as I would love to tell you that there was a method by which I got people to actually listen to my messages, there wasn't. Even today, each time I give a talk, a little voice in the back of my brain causes me to wonder how many more times will people find value in what I'm saying and how long it will be before the invitations stop coming. I have found that practicing anything does in fact make perfect, but it isn't everything. Having faith in yourself and putting yourself in the path of experiences and allowing them to find you is essential. I had no plans for my public speaking to extend any further than the two organizations at Troy High School, but because I believed in what I was saying, people listened and opened doors that not even I thought were possible.

With the end of my junior year at Troy High School approaching, my thoughts turned to the national FCCLA convention in Florida that July. Arrangements were being made to fly my mother and I there with the FCCLA advisor. As far as I was concerned, I had already won because my mother and Brew were more excited than I was. In fact, Brew was talking about how this trip to Florida was just a pit stop on the "Road to Washington," as he would call it. All throughout my high school career, Brew and I talked about how great it would be for me to speak on Capitol Hill. I promised Brew that if that opportunity ever presented itself I would take him with me. That, however, was a pipe dream at that point, but the last few days of school that year did bring with them an honor that will always be very special to me.

During our high school's Farewell Assembly before Commencement, our seniors ceremoniously walk in to the high school auditorium to be honored one last time by staff and students before they walk across the street to attend graduation practice. This day is for the seniors and honoring them, but there is a tradition where two outstanding junior students are recognized. The female recipient receives the Carson Award and one male recipient is conferred the Vesper Award, respectfully named after two former faculty members at Troy High School. In May of 2008, I was the recipient of the Vesper Award, which has been given at Troy High School since 1954 to the Outstanding Junior Male as chosen by the faculty of the school. Honorees are chosen based on their academics, civic involvement, and leadership qualities. The young man must also be someone of good character who has the respect of both students and teachers. I was honored to receive this award because not only is it steeped in the history of our school, this award was bestowed by the faculty and was a confirmation to me that I was an example of all those qualities that my mother and Brew, each in their different ways, passed on to me.

Two memories, in addition to receiving the award, stay with me from that day. The first memory is that the Mayor and Council President were there to watch me receive this distinguished award and, most importantly to me, my mother was there, and appropriately, Brew, was backstage, off to the side, so as I went back to my place in the auditorium, he was there ready with a hug and a big smile. This may seem like a small detail, but to me it meant everything because all I had done up to that point, the speeches, and the scholastic achievement, had been to make Brew proud of me. Looking back on it now, there was something in me, which needed to know that a man was proud of me. When I speak to student groups or interact with young people today, I meet boys who feel the same way I did. We all need to find the Scot Brewer in our lives, that role model who encapsulates the values we uphold and those attributes we see in ourselves.

With the end of the school year came the time to get ready for the national FCCLA Leadership Convention in Orlando, at which I would be presenting, "Diversity in American Legislation." It wasn't until right before I was due to leave in July that I realized just what a big deal this was. Contending for the title of "Best Competitive Speaker" in the Nation is not a position in which many teenagers find themselves and   Brew used this opportunity to impart another valuable lesson. He told me that the results of the competition were irrelevant. What mattered was that I was willing to go and do something that no one from my high school had ever done before. Put another way, it's not that we win or lose, it's that we made it to the game.

So often we make excuses for why we don't try things or step outside our comfort zone. Many talents lay dormant or never see the light of day because of fear of failure. I have to admit that as I was preparing to leave, these same doubts were going through my own mind. How was it, I wondered, that people from across the nation would be interested in anything I had to say about living with a disability and overcoming obstacles, let alone consider me for national recognition? As ever, Brew was on hand to remind me what was truly important. He told me that the only true way I could fail is I actually have to try. That gave me courage and taught me a lot about the true meaning of success. I learned that to be good or have anything, you have to be willing to try. You have to be bold enough to believe in yourself and put yourself in the path of people who will help you get to where you want to go. If all we can do is fail, we are ahead. Now mind you, I'm not suggesting we should not try our best and give one hundred percent in all we do, but what I am saying is that we should never be afraid to endeavor to try because even in the midst of our failures, we learn just how strong we really are. Positive things will come our way if we are only willing to try.

On July 13, 2008, my mother, FCCLA advisor, and I flew to Orlando, Florida so that I could deliver, what would be up to that point, the most important oration of my early public speaking career. It wasn't lost on me that I would be returning to the home state where I was born, where I was placed in an MH class in elementary school, the state where my father abandoned me. So much had changed since my move to Ohio. It seemed only appropriate that I had grown so much academically, cognitively, and emotionally, that I could come back to Florida to show I didn't need to be institutionalized, or segregated in a class in the back of a school, or have a nuclear family to be successful. I was back in Florida to show my oratory strengths and hopefully, to win some hardware! The national FCCLA competition is the state competition on steroids. There was something very surreal about the fact that the FCCLA National Convention where I would compete against over 2,000 students from all over America for the distinction of being named one of the best competitive public speakers in the nation, was held only two hours from the place I spent my early youth, where few people thought I would ever achieve much of anything. In those few moments after I presented, the irony of what I had come from and the reality of what was ahead was not lost on me.

Students from all across the country were there to compete in various leadership oriented competitions, public speaking being the most popular. I remember arriving very early that afternoon and being amazed at the number of students who were competing from all across the United States. At about 10 o'clock that evening, there was a meeting for all the students competing in the Illustrated Talk competition. It was explained to us that even though each talk required a PowerPoint or some sort of visual aid (hence the title Illustrated Talk), no screen would be provided by the national organization, and while the representative from the Troy, Ohio chapter did indeed have a PowerPoint, no one thought to bring the screen. So there we were, with less than 12 hours to go before speech time, and there was no projection screen. As my mother, FCCLA advisor, and I looked at each other in astonishment, my mom declared that she didn't care if she had to tie bed sheets to two poles, I was going to give that speech no matter what. As luck would have it, literally at the eleventh hour, my advisor heard that a group of students from the Nevada delegation would not be using their screen. Thankfully, they were more than happy to let me use it.

With that small hurdle behind me, the day for which I had spent months preparing finally arrived, competition day. I woke up very early that morning to sneak in one final practice of the talk in front of my mother, who at that point could have given the speech as well as I did. As the hour of the presentation approached, the importance of what was about to happen hit me. It wasn't that I was nervous, but I couldn't help but be taken aback by the fact that I was representing my school and state to the nation. If ever I wanted a speech to go well, it was now. The national FCCLA organization had overtaken the use of the entire resort for its leadership conference; thousands of people were about to hear my speech.

Just as I had at the State Convention in Ohio, once again I was in a room within the resort; this time with three judges from different states across the country. As I was preparing to give the talk, I remembered something Brew said to me before I left in another one of those teachable moments which had become so familiar to me and so central to my character. He said that, "while it is exciting to be recognized for a job well done, Michael, you are about to do something, the importance of which, goes far beyond the possibility of a national title". This was my opportunity to use my talent to bring about effective change in a positive way on a national scale. "Diversity in American Legislation" was more than just a speech, it was a platform of which I could be a voice for other people in similar circumstances. Brew's advice gave me pause to think about the true motives which drive the decisions in which we take part. There are any number of reasons why people get involved in the activities they do. Students may participate in extracurricular activities because they are passionate about certain organizations or sports, sometimes in the hopes that they will get scholarships or some kind of recognition for their efforts. Recognition and accolades for a job well done are important, people need pats on the back; the world can be a very bleak place without them. Brew's point, however, was that the desire to be noticed should never come before the desire to use our skills in order to be a positive influence in the lives of other people.

As I prepared to give the presentation in Florida, I wasn't so much thinking of it as a way to become a nationally awarded public speaker, but a medium through which I could do something that would leave a lasting impact and shed light on issues that many people take for granted or may not have considered. I think the three judges who heard the talk were a bit taken aback that someone with a disability could express their thoughts so cogently. They received the speech very well, much like it had been at the regional and state events in Ohio. At the national level, the interest wasn't just in the presentation, or the way in which I prepared for them, which drew interest, but the fact that someone with an obvious disability had made the choice to use what gifts he had to distinguish himself and be an influence for good in the process.

The judges asked questions about how I became interested in public speaking and the support system I had at home. So I told them about my mother and Brew and how he had inspired me to go places with my mouth. I found it surprising that the judges at this stage were so fascinated by the fact that someone in my position, (a disabled teenager) could speak so openly in front of others about such important issues. As one judge at Nationals put it, "I'm sure people don't always expect someone with a voice and thoughts like yours to come from someone sitting in that chair." I appreciated the honesty of that statement and I suppose it's true; people don't often associate being articulate and verbose with a disabled person.

But not every disabled person, or physically fit one for that matter, is raised by a woman who is possessed with an absolute almost single minded dedication to devote her life to caring for her child, while making sure that his life was not defined by other people's perception or notions of him. Every young person isn't blessed to have people like Chris and Gene who always have their back and inspires them to impact the lives of others; and certainly few students have had a mentor or brother like Brew, who replaced the memories of an absent father. As I was answering these questions from the judges in that room, I began to think of other young people who were in similar situations like mine, and how much untapped potential must exist within schools everywhere. I also realized that it only takes one teacher to make a difference in the life of a student.

If the waiting for scoring results at the regional and state levels had been difficult, at the national level it was almost impossible. The feedback on "Diversity in American Legislation" had been very complimentary even in the early stages, however, at the national level there was no way to gauge the skills of the other speakers because there were so many of them. As the time of the general session of the conference and the results drew near, I thought a great deal about my mother and the sacrifices she had to make to get me to this point. It had to have been a cathartic experience for her, especially because so many people told her that my options to be successful were limited at best. I was more excited about making her proud than the prospect of winning a medal. I was also filled with gratitude for Brew, the best "frother" that anyone could have asked for. As different as the football coach and the disabled public speaker seemed to be on paper, he gave me the courage to try. Any recognition this speech earned was due in large part to the time and effort he put into teaching me the true meaning of success.

The time came for the results portion of the conference. It wasn't until I saw the thousands of other students from FCCLA chapters from across the nation, all together, that I realized that this truly *was* a big deal. It seemed like an eternity before the Illustrated Talk competition results were announced. Once again, the waiting game was on. I sat and waited patiently as the bronze and silver medalists were called. Suddenly I felt as if I were one in a sea of thousands and the chances of my being awarded anything for this speech were nil. I was proud though, as I watched with my mother and advisor, because after all, the medal and the final analysis wasn't as important as the fact that I had finally found a skill that would, if used appropriately, define me in a way that was independent of my disability.

That is certainly how I felt during that national competition. All the positive vibes in the world, however, can't fix a deflated ego when one's name isn't called as a recipient of a public speaking medal. By my nature, I am an optimist who likes to see the glass as half full over being half empty. I try to focus my energy on what there is to smile about over what there is to worry about. I confess that these thoughts were somewhere in the recesses of my mind during the finale of the National FCCLA Leadership Convention. I reasoned that if I couldn't garner a silver or bronze medal than I was most assuredly going back to Troy empty handed. The gold never crossed my mind. Even this seemingly insignificant chain of thoughts that I had in those moments have taught me something. People can often quickly think of five negative thoughts before they can come up with something positive. That was certainly the case for me that day in Orlando. The fact that the speech had been given perfect scores at both the regional and state levels was irrelevant at this point. For me, the thought of achieving top scores at a national event was light years away from reality. What was an eighteen-year-old boy in a wheelchair, who was for all intents and purposes very new to public speaking, doing at a national competition? I quickly abandoned this line of thought and remembered Brew's words to me before I left. He said, "Wins and losses aren't as important as having played the game." Before I knew it, they were ready to reveal the speakers who earned gold medal top honors.

When my name wasn't called having received gold I was surprised at how disappointed I was not. It was a bit of an anticlimax, but I was thrilled to have come that far. As the last gold medalist returned to their seat, the National President of FCCLA announced that for the first time there was a student who achieved a perfect score in the Illustrated Talk competition. I was intrigued by that, but thought that person would have been from amongst the winners already announced. There was, after all, quite a cross section of students from across the United States who spoke about important issues like volunteerism, substance abuse, and the importance of education. "Diversity In American Legislation," while it discussed the vitally important issues that those with disabilities must face, really only applied to a certain section of our society, and there was no way, in my mind, that it could possibly have garnered the top honors.

So, to say that I was in a state of shock when I heard the words "Michael Ham from Troy, Ohio," was the understatement of the year. Everything seemed to be a blur as I moved up to the stage to accept the gold medal placed around my neck. The stage inside the auditorium of the resort was raised off the ground about five feet and a ramp had been placed at the side so that my wheelchair could access the stage. Once there, I couldn't see the audience below because of the lights, but I could hear applause. I found out later from my mother that the 4,000 strong audience rose to their feet for a standing ovation. In that moment, all I could focus on were the words of the FCCLA National President as he presented me with the medal. He said, "You realize that you have been named this year's best competitive speaker in the nation! Congratulations!"

Those words sent a chill down my spine. All the work, that faith that my mother put into me, and all the work that Brew, Gene, and Chris had done to guide me was paying off. As I received the well wishes of people representing FCCLA Chapters from virtually every state and territory, I kept expecting to wake up from a dream that seemed too good to be true. I went into sensory overload after the presentation. Thus, I don't remember much of the initial few hours after receiving the honor except for my mother's smile of pride, which I think she wore for several weeks after. I couldn't wait to get home and tell Brew. I knew that this distinction was as much his as mine.

Having someone in your corner (in addition to a parent) is just as wonderful as achieving something you have worked hard for. Having someone to share your joys with makes them mean more. Parental support is the driving force behind a young person's success. I know that there is no possible way that I could have ever achieved all I did without my mother's support and sacrifices. However, when a young person lacks a same sex influence, having someone like Brew at your side means the world. Most parents, certainly most mothers by design, give their children unconditional love, and Patricia Ham, without question, was the personification of that statement. But when a man like Brew who has meant so much to so many young men as a teacher, coach, and mentor sees something in you when he could have given his time to many others, it makes one want to try all the harder to be what they believe you can.

When we returned home to Ohio, congratulations poured in from so many people. It was very humbling and gratifying to know that so many people within my hometown were so proud of my achievement. Amidst the cards, letters, and phone calls the congratulations that meant the most to me was the one that came from Brew. If all he said was that he was proud of me that would have been worth all the effort that went into presenting "Diversity in American Legislation." But

Brew being Brew was ready with my next challenge. He reminded me of the prediction he made three years earlier when I was a freshman. He always said that he wanted to be there on the day that I became such a famous speaker that I would be invited to speak to the United States Congress. To Brew, you should never rest on your achievement for too long, but go forward and continue to be a positive influence.

At that time though, the interest in Troy's first national public speaker was intense. The rest of the summer in 2008 was spent speaking to organizations throughout Troy about my national FCCLA experience until the story crystallized into something approaching mythical status. Both the Troy and Dayton newspapers ran stories about the first Troy resident ever to win national recognition for writing speeches. The Ohio Department of Education even coined my talk, "The Perfect Speech" and sent one of their representatives to Troy to interview me. The attention that the national award brought with it was exciting. When I started speaking regularly, I really only had one goal for each talk and that was if it helped or gave courage to one person that heard it, all the work was worth it. In all these years that objective has never changed. Many people have asked me in the last decade if there is a secret formula to my method of public speaking. I feel as though I let them down when I tell them that my approach to presentations was really no secret at all and is really quite simple. Find something you are passionate about and speak it from your heart, that is the key to doing anything.

I learned this as early in my high school career from a teacher who was, in my mind, everything I could hope to be and ended up being everything to me. Brew will always have my love and respect for giving me the care and attention that I needed, making me realize that there was life beyond my disability and inspiring me to use my talents to help people. Above all, for teaching me that life is all about heart. Herein lies the fundamental importance of education. It isn't the facts, figures, or curriculum we take with us when we graduate; rather it's the people. The teacher who makes us excited to learn, the coach who pushes us to the limit so that we learn to believe in ourselves, or the mentor who becomes our father figure or brother and fills whatever other role we need at that time. For the students reading this, I wish you a teacher like Brew at least once in your life. To you who are teachers, may you be to your students what they need from you in that moment. Remind each one of them that you believe in them, care about their future, and will do all you can to help them be the best version of themselves.

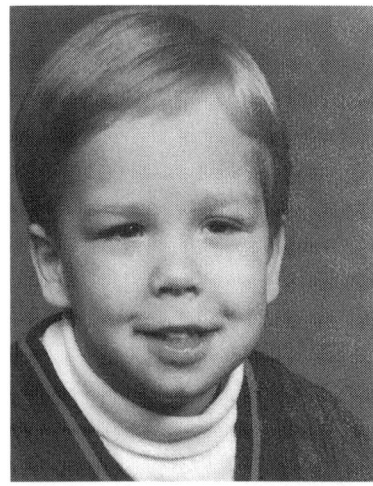

Left: Me, age 4, in Florida, where I was born.

All photographs are taken from Michael Ham's personal archives unless otherwise indicated.

Above: We moved to Ohio to be closer to my grandfather, Lowell Bodenmiller. Full of knowledge, he encouraged me to surround myself with good people.

Right: Chris Karnehm, my aide at the junior high.

Below: Gene Steinke - history teacher. I was his student aide at Troy Junior High School.

Left: Brew and me. Being his student aide for four years in high school was the mentoring I needed. As the most important person in my life, he has always had my back.

Mom was always my biggest supporter!

Here we are in May 2008, after the FCCLA state conference in Columbus. This trophy denoted I qualified to compete at the National Conference in Orlando in July!

Here is Mom at my graduation from Wright State University in 2013. This was the proudest day of her life. Her dedication to my education and well-being made this day possible.

After earning a perfect score on the Illustrated Talk competition at the FCCLA national competition in Florida, I earned a gold medal. Over a decade later, Evil "stole it" from Brew's classroom, I had it framed, and gave it to him on his birthday.

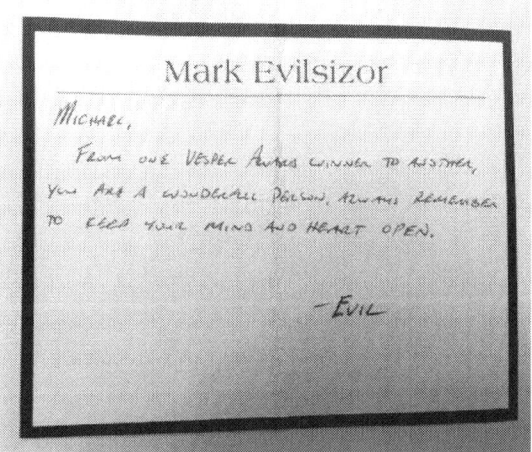

Top: My lunch buddy, and fellow Vesper Award winner, Mark Evilsizor. I still carry the congratulatory note he gave me every day in my dress shirt pocket.

Photo courtesy: Troy Chamber of Commerce.

In 2014, I was awarded the A. Robert Davis M.D. Memorial Outstanding Young Man of the Year Award. To say I was shocked to receive this award is an understatement. I hold the belief that awards aren't the reason why we should do good things.

Left to Right: Mayor Michael Beamish, Mr. Tom Funderburg, Assistant Director of the City of Troy, and Mr. Tom Dunn, Superintendent of the Miami County Educational Service Center.

Photo courtesy of Natalie Rohlfs and The Future Begins Today.

I have always believed it is important to give back!

In 2014, I became a board member for The Future Begins Today, a local non-profit organization that has provided mentoring, nurturing and scholarship programs to our local students for the past twenty-five years.

Above: I am passing out samples of our famous Strawberry Salsa at our Strawberry Festival. 100% of the proceeds of the sales of our salsa provide scholarship to college students. Visit *thefuturebeginstoday.org* to order some for yourself, it is delicious!

Photo courtesy of the Miami Valley Today (That's our Local Newspaper).

In November of 2016, I was elected to the Board of Education. This picture was taken at my swearing-in ceremony in January. Mom was sitting in the back of the room, supporting me, like always. As a board member, it is an honor for me to help the educators and students in Troy. Left to Right: Treasurer Jeff Price, President Doug Trostle, and myself.

Brad Rohlfs and I after I threw out the first pitch at a Dayton Dragons game. After Mom passed away, Brad picked me up every Sunday morning so I could go to church.

Brew and Gene Steinke shaped who I am by fostering my gifts and talents. As a student aide to both of them, I have seen firsthand how the dedication of educators will shape who their students are for a lifetime.

Family can take on many forms. Clarice Francis, my "surrogate" mom, accompanies me to as many speaking engagements as she can. This is from a presentation I gave to the Ohio Council for People with Disabilities, in Newark, Ohio.

Washington D.C.

In 2017, Brad, Brew, Chris and I travelled to Washington D.C. so I could speak to the Senate regarding STABLE accounts, which allow individuals with disabilities the opportunity to save and invest money without losing eligibility for certain public benefits programs. I was honored to be able to put my public speaking skills to good use and glad the guys could accompany me!
Top: (L to R) Brad, Scot, me, and Chris.
Right: Brad and I at Statuary Hall.

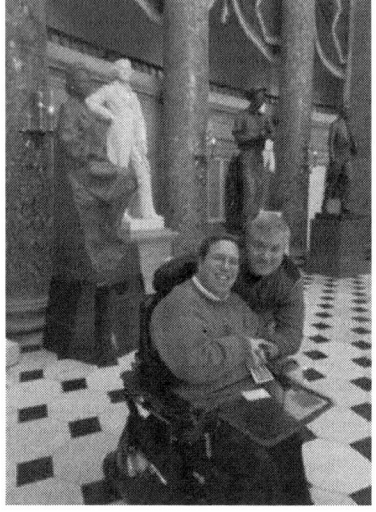

Brew and me: Brothers Forever

LESSON 4

Embrace the Grind

Senior year of high school is a time of mixed emotions for all young people. They are excited about beginning the next chapter of their lives, yet also have some trepidation about leaving what is familiar and safe for the harsh realities of adulthood and living independently. My senior year was no different; this was the period where I really had to think about the direction I wanted my future to take. I also learned the meaning of true independence and what it meant to embrace the grind.

Being a nationally awarded public speaker brings its own unique opportunities. Word travels fast in a small town and with the media coverage that the national speech received, by the time my final year of high school arrived, I earned the reputation for having a big mouth. Now, even service clubs and organizations outside of Troy were asking me to speak on a variety of issues from living with a disability and the importance of scholastic achievement to how to give an effective talk. I guess they figured that anyone who wins national recognition for speaking as a teenager, might know something about how to do it well.

I was grateful for each speaking engagement that I had because it gave me the chance to inspire others and do them some good while participating in something about which I am still very passionate. The ability to communicate with other people is a gift we should never take for granted.

The Ohio FCCLA organization asked if I would have any interest in being a state officer. This meant that during the school year, I would travel to different school districts and speak to their FCCLA chapters about the importance of taking a leadership role in the school and community. I was honored and humbled by the invitation and realized it was an amazing opportunity, but I chose to decline it. With it being my senior year, I wanted to spend my time focusing on what lay ahead for me. I was applying to college that fall and knew that was going to take a lot of preparation once I was accepted. But more than anything, I wanted to stay with Brew during my last year of high school. As a state officer, I would have to be away from Troy High School quite a bit and would have to forfeit the ability to be Brew's student aide. That was a title that I wasn't about to relinquish until it was absolutely necessary. I realized I still needed some mentoring before I headed off to the great unknown, college.

Just before the start of school, my final year, my mother picked up my course schedule. At the end of the previous year, I signed up for elective courses to take when school resumed. One of the courses I signed up for was Economics. If I am being honest, I have to admit that my motive behind taking this particular elective within the social studies department was less than academic; I knew that Brew would be teaching it. Though I had been his student aide, to that point I hadn't actually been his student. When she saw my schedule, my mother called me to say that not only had I gotten into Brew's class, but later in the day I had a study hall, which meant that I could be his aide once more. Christmas had come early as far as I was concerned.

It was just as well that it had. I was facing some very important decisions my senior year and needed Brew's influence more than ever. Beyond that, I had made the choice to compete in the FCCLA competition, as well as, focus my time on the Troy High School Speech and Debate Team. As ever, Brew was always on hand to be a captive audience to practice my speeches before and after school and build me up as the speaking engagements to different groups became more prevalent. I treasured each opportunity that came, but I couldn't help but wonder how long it would last before audiences would get bored with me. The messages were good in themselves because they covered a wide range of issues and Troy High School was very supportive of my speaking especially since many of the talks were over lunchtime and during the school day, so I did not have to miss valuable class time.

The end of 2008 was spent crafting a presentation for the high school Speech and Debate team and applying to colleges. The speech team took a lot of time, unlike FCCLA, where I could pick the topic that I wanted to present, whereas the subject matter for the Speech and Debate team was assigned to me at random. This was a challenge for me, but one I accepted. I always think it's good to force oneself out of our comfort zone. Though it can be intimidating when we try something new, it allows us to test our limits. It also ensures that we never become complacent about the talents we possess. It's easy when some call you one of the best student speakers, or the best anything in the nation, to think you know all there is to know about public speaking. Being truly great at something means understanding that there is always something we don't know. Learning is a lifelong process, and sometimes we don't know what we don't know.

I was very interested to see the topic that was assigned to me. Each year the districts of Speech and Debate teams would generate a list of topics to present about in the Original Oratory competition; each one was about issues that are important to our society. The subject that was assigned to me was, "My Role in Honoring America's Veterans." That took me aback because it was never a topic in which I thought to speak. I felt honored to be able to bring attention to an issue that is so important, but not often talked about. This is also where having a history teacher as your mentor pays off! My participation in the speech team was somewhat different than that of FCCLA, aside from being assigned a prompt, the schools at which I competed were further away. The closest school was Oakwood, which was about 25 minutes away from Troy. Most weeks from December to March, I would board a school bus at 6:00 A.M. in the Junior High parking lot, which would take me to schools in Gahanna, Oakwood, and Spring Creek, on successive Saturday mornings. When I started my tenure on the team, we were a small group of three students and as time progressed I became the lone member with the advisor. Public speaking isn't a skill that everyone is comfortable with and some don't fully appreciate how daunting it can be to speak and present your thoughts in front of an audience until you actually do it.

Like the speech competitions I had participated in previously with FCCLA, the atmosphere of each Speech and Debate competition was very formal. Shirts and ties for males were a requirement. Thankfully, I had Brew to tie my ties for me on the Friday before each tournament. I am not physically able to tie them, he did it so that I would be ready for the next day. This became our pregame, or pre-speech, ritual. I would go into his classroom on a Friday, he would prepare my tie, or uniform, for game day, and then I was prepared and ready for battle. He would make sure that not only the message was impactful, but also that the messenger had everything he needed to deliver it well.

The Original Oratory competitions were held in the classrooms of the school that was hosting the tournament. Another difference between this experience and the other speech events in which I participated was that speakers were divided into groups of ten, so in addition to the three judges, each student spoke in front of the others in their group. This was a daunting task because I was used to presentations being private, virtually sequestered from the others. It is certainly difficult to stack yourself up against students who are just as passionate and adept at speaking as you think you are. One aspect separated me from my cohort of presenters. While we all spoke on vital issues to our world, my peers began in very theatrical ways. Some used music while others crafted very creative skits with the goal of grabbing the audience's attention. Without a doubt, this was a very effective tool, nevertheless, I employed a different method to my presentation style. I have always maintained, rightly or wrongly, that speeches should not be theatrical. Drama should be left to thespians who know how to do it well.

Speaking from the heart had been ingrained in me for so long that it has become a part of every talk I give even today. My practice was to begin with a story about the people or a person impacted by the subject in which I was speaking. In "Diversity in American Legislation," I began with highlighting the life of President Franklin D. Roosevelt who, despite the challenges of polio, led the country through World War II. As part of this presentation about honoring our veterans, I spoke about the patients at Walter Reed Military Medical Center and the substandard care they receive from the government. I believe when you are bringing attention to serious issues, it is essential to put a face to it. People don't pay attention to concepts, facts or figures; they are impressed by them up to a point, but too many of them make the topic unreal. Each time, I referenced an individual person or group of people, either from research or my own experience. This method of bringing light to the issues I was speaking about seemed to resonate with the audiences and speech judges who heard it.

I was assured that the tactic paid off as I was chosen to advance to the next round to represent Troy at other speech tournaments throughout Ohio; even being chosen as State Alternate at one of them.   Despite the challenges of days that began before the sun came up and ended long after it went down, and the battles with laryngitis (unlike FCCLA where speeches were given only once, speech tournaments required three rounds) it was all worth it if I could inspire or empower one person sitting in an audience to live their best life.

If the truth were told, I used the speech team and FCCLA as a distraction that year. I threw myself into the speech process and making sure that I finished academically strong. This sounds like just the right way to secure a successful future - and indeed it is. However, I think I was so busy with speaking in the later part of 2008 and in the beginning of 2009 that when it was time to apply to colleges, I was astonished at how fast time was passing me by. It was time to start planning for life after Troy High School. I was apprehensive to do it because that meant leaving the safety of the school and the care of my teachers at Troy High School who had been so supportive and made my success to that point possible.

As I look back on it now, I realize as a student what a unique position I was in. Not only was I a nationally recognized competitive speaker, but most importantly, I was fortunate that I had a unique relationship with some of the faculty at Troy High School. What made my high school experience unique to that of many others, was, oddly enough, the way I spent my lunchtime. Brew and some of the other male teachers who sat at the teacher's table asked me to join them. I got more education about the meaning of life than I could have ever wished for. These guys brought me such joy at a time when I needed it so much. During these half hour periods I got to know the man that would become my "Lunch Buddy."

Mark Evilsizor teaches World History in the classroom next to Brew's. No one can matriculate through the hallways of Troy High School for long before the man affectionately referred to as "Evil" makes his presence known. The first thing you notice about Evil is his booming voice. When I was helping Brew as a student aide in his classroom, our joke used to be that he team taught with Evil because he could be clearly heard when Brew left his door open. I had no possible way of knowing that the person behind that rousing expressionism would be one of the people that would play a key role in the continuation of my success. On several occasions, I found myself ducking into his classroom to hear portions of his lessons just before lunch. Evil has an ebullient personality and brings the most incredible level of passion to everything he does, especially teaching.

Every teacher brings with them a philosophy of education which guides their particular style of instruction and the way they interact with their students. Gene's philosophy gave me my start by bringing out my talents and encouraging me to be bold enough to give public speaking a try. Brew's defined for me the way a man was supposed to live by showing me that the essential element of success was caring about people and using our skills to make a difference for the people we come in contact with. Now here was Evil, inspiring me with his oft repeated mantra, "Enthusiasm is Contagious."

Being in Evil's presence is akin to the excitement that one experiences when they start school or a new job for the first time. Whether it's role playing the points of feudalism or discussing how the dangers of prejudice led to the Holocaust, Evil has a way of making the listener just as passionate about what he's saying, without them fully realizing exactly why. That is what underpins the qualities of not only a great teacher, but also a great leader. I wanted to be around Evil because he has the ability to meet people where they are while instilling in them a thirst for learning.

Truly joy filled people are those who bring excitement to every aspect of their own life. This is the most valuable life lesson I learned from Evil. Though he was never technically my teacher, I hope that a bit of his personality has rubbed off on me. For three years, Evil and I shared the same lunch period and I would often go to the cafeteria and eat with he and other teachers at the "teacher table". No other student in Troy High School history has ever been given that privilege. I was in a very unique position during my high school years for a number of reasons, not the least of which is because of how I spent my lunch periods. During this time, I learned more about life than most students could have bargained for or could ever be gained from textbooks. Sitting next to Evil was an experience. No topic was off limits at that table; looking back I realize how unorthodox it must have seemed to substitutes and other visitors to the school who might have seen this student sitting with a group of teachers in the middle of the cafeteria.

I admire Evil because he was always willing to challenge me. To him, the ability to speak and debate was a great skill; however, he argued that it was just as important to know why we hold the beliefs we do. Evil made a very special impact on me because he taught me the value of the why. It isn't enough to take a position on an issue, but to understand why you hold it, even if it means challenging your own thought process. Evil taught me to think and put logic behind the words. Countless students have counted on Evil as a coach where he would assist them in making sure they were conditioned to play football, basketball, baseball, or golf. Nevertheless, the brain is the most important muscle within the human body and I will always be grateful that in the middle of everything else he was doing during those years, he took the time to whip the most important muscle in *my* body into shape, by teaching me to use it in a whole new way.

That is why I asked him to advise me on the talks I gave. I figured that if anyone would know how to captivate an audience, it was Evil. He gave me a handwritten note when I was voted by Troy High School's faculty and named the Outstanding Junior Male, called the Vesper Award (named after Dale Vesper, respectively), in May of 2008. Incidentally, the same honor was bestowed upon him in 1992, so I was honored that he took the time to congratulate me in a personal way by writing me a handwritten note that I carried with me, in the left breast pocket of my dress shirt, through that last year of high school, all throughout college, and years afterward until it practically disintegrated from years of me looking at it for instant inspiration. It said, "From one Vesper Award winner to another, you are a wonderful person, always remember to keep your mind and heart open." While the bit about me being a "wonderful person" is debatable at best, having an open mind and heart has been imprinted in my brain ever since. I always knew that was the best credo to adopt, but Evil, with his enthusiastic way of living, showed me *how* to live it.

My relationship with Evil taught me that inspiration can come in the most unexpected ways. Like Brew, Gene, and Chris before him, Evil and I were quite different at the surface. Not only were, Evil, Brew, Chris, and Gene Varsity football coaches at our Division 1 Ohio high school (a really big deal if you follow national high school football), but Evil was also politically left of center, which is diametrically opposite of my own viewpoint. However, Evil showed me that people who think differently than we do are oftentimes one of our greatest gifts. Can you imagine how boring the world would be if everyone thought the same way we do? It is important to have a set of values which guide your life, nevertheless, as we are deciding what those are, we should listen to all sides of every issue before arriving at an opinion. Evil showed me how to bring passion to everything I did. During those lunch periods, Evil demonstrated that the best speakers listen first. They listen to people's hardships, their joys, their hopes and dreams; then and only then, Evil contended, can you speak intelligently enough to inspire others.

A common trait that Brew, Gene, Chris, Evil, and the other individuals within this book all share is the ability to tell me what I need to hear when I need to hear it. As a society, we have become very soft; we feel it necessary to surround ourselves with "yes people". We all know the type: those people who tell us what we want to hear. The bonds that I have formed with the people discussed within these pages, each in their own way, have shown me that the people that truly love you don't tell you what you want to hear, they tell you what you need to hear no matter how hard it is.

This unfiltered approach to mentoring was invaluable to me at this particular moment in my life. It isn't easy deciding the direction of one's life under normal circumstances, but when you have physical challenges it requires lots of extra planning. To that end, I decided to truly focus on my career goals during the second semester of my senior year. It so happened that Troy High School offered a course which allowed its students to spend two days a week job shadowing someone whose career path they intended to follow. I always had a political bent to my thinking and wanted a career where I could combine my desire to help people with my ability to communicate. The political and legislative process fascinated me. From a very early age people always told me that I had a future in politics. However, a trip to Washington D.C. in the latter part of the first semester of my senior year changed my thought process.

I was selected to attend the National Youth Leadership Forum on Foreign Policy and National Security in October of the previous year in Washington D.C. Four hundred and thirty-five students from across the United States were chosen to participate in this simulation which centered around an oil crisis in the Caspian Sea Region. During the course of the week, we learned about diplomacy and the American political process. The participants vied for different cabinet positions within a mock presidential cabinet tasked with taking the diplomatic skills we learned throughout the week and applying them to the oil crisis. My peers chose a burgeoning public speaker from a Midwestern town in Ohio, me, to be their President of the United States for the week. It was my job to approve the choices made by the cabinet and make the speeches which delineated the administration's plans. Here again I was able to use my public speaking ability on a national scale, when I had to delineate for the other students how it was we were going to use what we had learned to handle the crisis. This was a once in a lifetime experience which I was grateful to be part of and it taught me something very valuable.

Just as I had thought as an eighth grader, the policies which trickle down from the federal level don't truly impact people on a daily basis and as a result I concluded that local government was where I could use my skills to make an impact on people. When it was time to take the Career Mentorship elective class during the first semester of my senior year, I requested to job shadow the Mayor of Troy, Mr. Michael Beamish and the Superintendent of Troy Schools, Mr. Tom Dunn. The Mayor always supported my public speaking and had kept in contact with me, offering ideas for talks and providing speaking engagements for me. He readily agreed to allow me to job shadow him so once a week he would trade vehicles with my mother, take her handicap accessible van and pick me up from school so that I could be a part of his afternoon activities.

As part of the experience, Mayor Beamish arranged for me to have tours of the various municipal departments. Each week we would visit a different facility. This, more than anything else, solidified in my mind that this was the career I wanted to pursue. I realized from during my previous job shadowing that local government impacts the lives of people on a daily basis and now I was seeing just how true that was. With every tour, I began to understand that the police station, fire department, water plants, and maintenance facility weren't stand-alone institutions in themselves, but an essential part of an intricate mechanism that was the City of Troy, whose mission it was to serve the citizens of the community while providing the best quality of life possible.

I knew I wanted to study Public Administration in college, but I wanted a wider sense of what made a community successful. Education was stressed so much in my home by my mother that I wanted a better understanding of what it takes to run a school district. Each Wednesday afternoon I would stroll from the high school parking lot to the Board of Education office where I would shadow Mr. Dunn, the Superintendent of Troy City Schools. These sessions did much more than expose me to the inner workings of the school district; unlike most career exploration programs of its kind, I wasn't the only one asking the questions. Mr. Dunn had questions for me too.   I had met him in 2005 when he was named Troy's new Superintendent and I was a freshman contemplating a public speaking role. Later, Mr. Dunn had been impressed when I won the national award for speaking from FCCLA and invited me to give the presentation to the Board of Education. He wanted to know about me and how it was that I stayed so positive in the midst of the challenges that I had to face. I told him about Brew, Chris, Gene, Evil and the juxtaposition of experiences between where I had come from in Florida and all I had accomplished since coming to Troy. Mr. Dunn said that my situation is one of the reasons why he agreed to participate in the job shadowing/ mentorship program. I was the first student in my school district of 4,500 to be granted an opportunity to have regular one-on-one meetings with the Superintendent.

I believe Mr. Dunn saw the mentorship program as a chance to be reminded of what education is really all about and why he got involved with it in the first place. Superintendents, by the nature of their job, don't always interact with the students in their district, and when they do it's not always for the most positive of reasons.

On paper, if you looked strictly at my scholastic record, beyond being on an Individual Education Plan, (which allowed me to have extended time and a scribe during tests exams because of my disability), there was nothing that would have ever given any indication that I needed anything beyond the norm because I was never "in trouble." And although one would never have known by my math grades, my scholastic ability was, as a whole, above average. My time with Mr. Dunn confirmed that this is the most essential function of a teacher: that is, to make all their students feel that there is something in them that makes them uniquely special, while inspiring them to relentlessly pursue their passion.

One day in the beginning of 2009, Brew asked me when I was going to use what I was learning and apply to college. After some discussion, we settled that I would apply to the Ohio State University and Wright State University in Dayton, which was a premier school for students with disabilities. I was accepted into both schools, but decided to attend Wright State because of their Disability Services program. Beyond that, the campus was a half hour from Troy so my support system was reasonably close if things went astray.

I enrolled in the College of Liberal Arts and declared my major in Urban Affairs. To me that sounded like a great title for a soap opera; in actuality, it was a very educated way of saying that I was going to study local government administration. If applying, getting accepted, and declaring a major was easy, the next steps were like a cold snowball in my face. In February of 2009, my mother and I went for a tour of Wright State and a meeting with the Physical Support Supervisor within the Disability Services department. Wright State had a mandate at the time which required all physically disabled freshmen to live on campus for their first two years. It was explained to us that as a student at Wright State, I would be taking a course which would teach me how to manage the four student personal assistants who would be in charge of my personal care. I would learn how to: schedule, recruit, interview, hire, and when called for, dismiss them. These skills would serve me after college as I prepared to live independently.

When I asked how these personal assistants or "PAs" would be chosen, I was told that most of them were international students, primarily from India, who considered it an honor to care for the disabled. Further on in the meeting, the person from disability services said there would be a bit of a language barrier by virtue of the fact that they were international students. Therefore, it would be necessary to write down my needs, at least to start. It was at that moment a feeling of what I can only describe as abject terror came over me.

How, I wondered, was it possible that with not even a basic understanding of the English language, someone could be expected to care for a disabled person with only a week's training before the school year started? The Wright State campus itself impressed me because of how accessible it was. Every door to each of the buildings had an automatic handicapped friendly button. It was somewhat fortuitous that I would be attending the same university and traverse the same underground tunnels into which Chris and I found ourselves lost five years earlier. For all of the amazing attributes that Wright State had, I couldn't shake the fear about how I was going to get personal care. Many people don't realize that someone in my position is reliant on other people for the most basic of physical needs including: dressing, bathing, and other activities of daily living, like cleaning my dorm room and helping me make sure that my class materials for the day were in order. Up to this point my mother had been virtually the only one to give me this type of care. The thought of turning it over to someone else for the first time was an adjustment for both of us.

The ride back to Troy on that cold February day was very quiet; without acknowledging it, my mother and I chose to focus on the positive. After all, I *had* come a long way from those early days in Florida in a classroom for students with special needs. Moreover, I knew that this was so important to Mom, it was what she had planned for despite Todd and the educational professionals in Florida telling her that college was not an option for me. So whatever reservations we both may have harbored in that moment, we each kept them to ourselves because we both knew how important this was to the other.

When I returned to Troy High School the next day, I shared about my visit to Wright State with Brew. He was also the one person I shared my concerns with. Brew had always been my safe place. Today, young people demand safe places in schools and even in the workplace and I suppose that as a teenager that is one of the many roles that Brew filled for me. He provided me a safe place to talk about difficult things, however, unlike today's "safe places," he never told me what I wanted to hear, but instead what I needed to hear. This time was no different. I told him about my concerns about the care I would get. Everyone who goes to college goes into it with a bit of trepidation, but in addition to the worries of adjusting to a new way of life, the first taste of independence, living away from home, and scheduling the right courses, I had to think about how I was going to coordinate my personal care. What would happen if they didn't show up on time? How would I communicate with the international students who were only basically trained on the essentials of caregiving? All these questions and more were on my mind as I unloaded on Brew in his room after school.

He listened intently and shared many of my concerns. As ever, though, Brew used this as a moment to present another life lesson. He said that it was perfectly normal to be nervous or even afraid, going on to say that he would have thought there was something wrong with me if I wasn't nervous about the next step of my educational journey. Nevertheless, I had to give this opportunity a fair chance. I had come too far to turn back now. Most importantly, he told me that nothing in this life worth having ever comes easily. At that particular moment, I was faced with another choice to make like so many before it in my life. I could let fear overcome me, depriving myself of the future and opportunities that I had worked so hard for, or I could embrace the grind of the situation and press on.

Embracing the grind is an idea that is foreign to many people today. We live in a society that encourages us to avoid what is difficult or challenging or uncomfortable in favor of that which is easy or convenient. When we shy away from challenges we rob ourselves of the ability to grow. I often think of how diamonds or gemstones must endure a great degree of pressure, heat, and cutting to become the valuable objects they are. That same analogy can be applied to all of us when we have obstacles we must face. How many of us have faced the prospect of going through something very difficult, we come out the other side and realize that the experience, as awful as it was, made us better? This is the situation I found myself in as I prepared to graduate from Troy High School.

Leaving Brew and the safety net he provided for me was intimidating. Spending four years of your life learning from someone you respect and admire as much as the woman that brought you into the world makes it daunting and scary to think about. But as Brew himself reminded me, just because I was going to college, did not mean he was going anywhere. One day shortly before graduation, I asked Brew what I would do if something bad happened while I was having my first taste of life on my own. As he had always done, he assailed my apprehension by reassuring me that no matter what, he would be there for me. One of my most coveted possessions is a book he gave me as a graduation present about the founding principles of democracy. On the inside cover he wrote the words, "Remember, I've got your back!" We often said this idiom to one another at different times; I had no way of knowing at the time how much that phrase would continue to be a reality.

One challenge that all incoming college students share, regardless of disability, is how to pay for it. Upon graduation, I received about $1,000 in scholarships which was a far cry from the $40,000 I needed. Knowing that her contribution would be nominal, and that my ability to take out loans would be limited, my mother was tirelessly helping me research funding opportunities when in early June 2009, she stumbled upon a television commercial advertising that this particular station, known as Dayton's CW, would be holding an essay contest for a four-year tuition scholarship to Wright State, valued at $35,000. My mother saw it as an answer to prayer. I, on the other hand, was somewhat skeptical.

I knew that Dayton's CW had been awarding scholarships for a number of years and had often remarked how it would be wonderful to receive that award. But as I said to my mother, the likelihood of the selection committee choosing my submission out of the 500 they received were slim to none. I suddenly discovered there was a drawback to being named a nationally awarded public speaker when my mother reminded me that just a year ago, I was chosen as number one in a contest of over two thousand across the nation. She reasoned this would be easy in comparison to that, besides if we venture nothing we gain nothing. Nothing hurts the pride of someone known for speaking and debating than when his parent presents an argument he can't refute! The prompt of the essay was *How a College Education Will Impact Me and My Community.* I wrote about how we all have an obligation to do what we can to help others. Mentorship had shown me how to live out that mission and how earning a degree would enable me to use my skills to help others on a professional level. Writing the piece was easy, keeping it to the two-hundred-word limit was not. Thankfully, Superintendent Dunn was a good editor and was able to pare down the original five-hundred-word draft to make it meet specifications, without sacrificing any of the core message.

I mailed the scholarship application with the essay to the television station thinking that chances were minimal that I would hear anything from them. In the meantime, I turned my attention to preparing to be a college student. This meant attending freshman orientation, scheduling classes, and making sure I knew what belongings I was taking with me. These are thoughts that every incoming college student has, but me being who I am guarantees that I can't ever do anything in the traditional way. In addition to the standard activities that all students undertake, I had to figure out how my care was going to get paid for because the university wouldn't pay for the care that I was going to receive. Naturally, I was responsible for reimbursing the school. I found out about an organization known as the Bureau of Vocational Rehabilitation. Their mission was to empower people with disabilities to acquire the skills necessary to find gainful employment. After an initial consultation and several evaluations, BVR consented to pay for my room, board and books. I was getting ever more nervous about how the tuition would be covered when I took a call at the end of June.

It was the Dayton's CW television station wishing to inform me that I had been selected as a finalist in their essay contest and requesting that I come to visit the station so that the winner could be chosen. As one of the station employees was giving me instructions on what time to be there and where to go, I remember thinking that this had to be some kind of joke. Thankfully, I didn't share that passing thought with Kelly, the page at the TV Station who called me that day, because a joke it was not. My mother was in a state of what I can only describe as elation; her plan was coming together. At this point I had to play the role of balloon pricker. While I was ecstatic to be one of the finalists, I reminded her that I was merely a finalist, a point that puzzled me. I wondered how they would actually choose the recipient of the scholarship. No details were given about the selection process, after all, there are only so many ways the winner of an essay contest is chosen outside of the content of the writing itself.

I envisioned there would be some committee or group of people who might ask some series of questions of the finalists, and choose the winner based on the answers that we gave. I began trying to surmise what questions they could ask and craft answers based on my experiences in high school and plans for the future and how I would impact the world around me upon the acquisition of my degree. On a Friday morning toward the end of June, my mother and I drove to the television station in Dayton, Ohio, where we were met by Kelly, the station page, who warmly welcomed us and showed the group to a well-furnished sitting area where we were told to wait as the other finalists arrived. The only instructions given about how the day would proceed is that all the finalists would be sequestered from one another.

Minutes seemed to pass like hours during this holding period. I tried to focus my attention on the answers I would give. Finally, Kelly the page came back and informed us that all the finalists were in place, but before it was time to begin, she was going to give my entourage and me a tour of the studio. While I was appreciative of her kindness, I was less than enthused about the idea of prolonging the wait to the main event. I was impressed with how such a small TV station in Dayton, Ohio, could keep up with the latest technology. As we turned the corner, Kelly explained that we were about to enter the main studio where the final contest would be held.

The first thing I remember upon going into the studio were the very bright lights that one would imagine in a TV studio. What surprised me was that instead of the other "finalists", I saw balloons, men in shirts and ties, and a huge green screen behind which Kelly instructed me to position myself. As my mother and I looked puzzled at one another, the general manager of the CW approached me. "Michael" he said, "we have been a little deceitful with you; you aren't a finalist in the contest." "Oh?", I said, rather taken aback. "No, you are the winner!!" He handed me a huge cardboard check reminiscent of the ones given by the

Publishers Clearinghouse to one of their lottery winners. From that moment on, the rest of the day went on in sort of a blurry haze, much of which I don't remember, save for the congratulations of everyone in that room, most of whom were the corporate sponsors of the scholarship. The smile on my mother's face lasted the rest of the day. The one question I asked was if there were no finalists, what was the point of sending us to the holding room? Kelly said that was to give time for the sponsors and the Assistant Provost of Wright State to arrive and get into place. They wanted to surprise me, and indeed they had.

On the ride home, I still couldn't quite comprehend what had happened. The final barrier which stood between me and the college education that seemed so improbable to so many just a decade prior, was removed. Any sane person would have been excited and overjoyed at the idea of a long worked for goal becoming a reality, and make no mistake that IS how I felt. However, as I look back on it now, I realize there was an element of uneasiness in me. Sometimes when we finally achieve that which we have always wanted, that in itself can be scary. Whatever doubts I had subsided when I remembered a fundamental truth about life; that is, no one goes his way alone. I wasn't just doing this for me, I was also doing it for my mother whose dedication helped make the scholarship a possibility. Moreover, of all the students that Brew impacted, for some reason he chose to allow me to hang around and for me to soak up his particular brand of success, which is now so much a part of who I am. I was ready to embark on this next phase of my life because it was my way of giving something back for the time that my mother, Brew, and the other guys in the inner circle put into me. It was the only "Thank You" that I felt was appropriate. These guys had shown up for me day after day. They supported and nurtured me and because of them, I was ready to leave the nest and "fly" to the college appropriately named, "Wright" State University, in honor of Orville and Wilbur Wright.

The summer of 2009 flew by as we prepared to have everything ready for my transition to college. Before I knew it, September 2nd arrived and it was move in day. I was full of mixed emotions. I was excited about the prospect of what lay ahead, nervous about living on my own for the first time and the standard of care I would receive, but more than anything, I was very cognizant of the fact that I wasn't the only one I was doing this for. This was the most monumental day for my mother. She and my grandfather, the only person on either side of my family who supported her devotion to me, moved me into my dorm room. I was full of mixed emotions, part of me was excited about embarking on a new chapter of my life. Coupled with the normal apprehensions that every incoming college student must face, were concerns about the manner in which my personal care would be provided, and whether these people who weren't much older than I was would be able to provide for my needs with little training.

These fears subsided when I thought for a brief moment about how Mom had raised me single handedly, sacrificing her marriage, financial security and even at one point having her fitness as a parent called into question. One of the only memories I have of Todd's family is that during the divorce they called Child Protective Services on Mom when she refused to place me in an institution; they said she was depriving me of appropriate care. Needless to say, the CPS caseworker ruled in Mom's favor and even commended her efforts on her devotion toward me and my care. She never said, so I have often wondered if, when I started college, she had the urge to go back to all those people who said it would never happen, and give them the loudest, "Told you so!" that anyone ever heard.

Starting university showed me that when you and I do anything good (or bad) it reflects on the people who support and believe in us. I was doing this for the small, but loyal group of people who helped make this opportunity a reality. They invested themselves into me; now was the time for me to give them a return on that investment. As we got everything situated in room 138 of Hamilton Hall, we met my four personal assistants. Navid and Joshi were from India, Kohto from South Africa, and Jacob was a local student from the Dayton area. As instructed by the Office of Disability Services, Mom and I wrote out my daily routine for the caregivers to follow. With the bustle of everything that moving into a college campus brings with it, the time for my mother and grandfather to go home snuck up on me. She was trying to hold in her emotion as she prepared to leave. Just before she left she took one last look at the dorm room she spent the day preparing. Mom said the room looked good, but in her mind it was missing something. She pulled out of her tote bag an 8x10 framed photograph of Brew, saying that she had it since early summer, but there was never a right time to give it to me.

I laughed and said that she had made an interesting gift choice. Mom said that there was a reason behind this particular memento. She told me, very rightly, that I was a visual person who was going to need something to look at when circumstances became difficult at school. This photograph would remind me of the lessons that Brew taught me and the fun he brought with them. I was fortunate that my mom understood this, because although I would commute home each weekend, the four years ahead would be a testing ground for everything that would come after them.

In terms of the academics, save for the faster pace, I didn't find college all that different from high school, especially since most of what I learned in the first year and a half of college was very much a review of what I learned at Troy High School. Though I realized I wasn't any better at math in college than at any another time in my scholastic career, I think I was supposed to glean more differences than I truly did. This was made evident to me when I saw on my schedule a course for disabled people with the goal of teaching us how to be disabled in college. While I found the lessons on study skills and time management very helpful, I found that being disabled at the university level wasn't much different from what I had experienced throughout my life, at least not with respect to my studies.

The differences were exposed outside the classroom. I knew the university experience was going to be the first test of living on my own and it was certainly a baptism by fire. As soon as my mother and grandfather left campus on move in day, the enormity of the situation was surreal. This was it! I met with the four personal assistants and established a routine, deciding who was going to take the morning shift and get me up from bed, dressed, and bathed in the morning and who would assist me at night and help with my bedtime routine. Jacob caught on pretty quickly and I learned he was going to be the good one.

Joshi, Navid, and Kotoh were very well intentioned and asked questions. Things started out relatively well, while writing my routine every day took some getting used to, I was handling it. The biggest challenge came in the mornings. For the first few weeks everything went well, Jacob took the morning shift and did well; he was always on time and wasn't at all apprehensive about taking on the task of caregiving. He was a nursing major who, like me, was an incoming freshman. Part of the morning routine was transferring me from the bed to the chair, which could be rolled into the shower. Caring for me was a bit more involved than many of my disabled counterparts. A lot of the other students with handicaps had portable lifts which could transition them relatively easily. I, on the other hand, was not in a position to have one of those. My left hip is dislocated, both of them were displaced at birth, so when I was six years old they were surgically put back in their sockets. At the age of ten, just before Todd left, he re-dislocated my left hip as he was trying to remove me from a rented car he hired to transport me to a nursing home without my mother's consent. Luckily, admitting a minor to a care facility required the consent of both parents. Someone tipped off my mother that Todd was trying to remove me from the home and she met us at the facility and took me back to our home. An x-ray during a doctor's appointment days later confirmed that the hip was in fact dislocated once again.

Medical professionals later concluded that spasticity was the probable cause of the dislocation. For my mother's sake and to keep the peace within our home, I never corrected their hypothesis. It was also decided that because of the deterioration of my lungs, brought on by my disability, surgery on my hip was out of the question. This made the care that I was getting at Wright State all the more challenging. It is immensely difficult to lift 200 pounds of dead weight (I am told) and all the more difficult when the caregiver is short in stature and nearly half my size. Under these conditions, complications are bound to arise. In fact, I was dropped on the floor of my dorm room seven times that first year when I was being cared for by fellow students. They didn't do it intentionally, but I also wonder if they fully understood the expectation and demands placed on caregivers. Instead of placing the shower chair next to the bed, they would try to carry me across the room and only make it about half way. The best optimist can find the good in the most impossible situations; I have subscribed to that line of thinking and my experiences at Wright State was no exception. I at least got a shower, albeit with some additional bumps and bruises.

I learned two very important lessons from the challenges pertaining to my care. The first is that the linoleum floor is cold at 5:30 in the morning. Thanks to Mom, Brew's picture came in handy and served just the purpose for which she intended. Each time they dropped me, I would look at Brew's picture, which I kept on the shelf. As Navid would get the janitor to come and lift me off the floor, my first thought was that there must be an easier way to get an education, and instead of a B.S. degree they should give me a purple heart to match my backside! I made a conscious decision in that moment that if I could endure Todd's physical abuse, abandonment, and the perceptions of others, even in my own "family," I could endure this temporary trial. I had come too far to quit now. Seeing Brew's framed photograph gave me the strength I needed to get up off the floor one more time. The second lesson I learned was that anyone who is challenged with a disability has to be an advocate for themselves. The mistake I made was that with every drop on the floor and every time I chose to stay on campus during the weekend and was left in my chair all weekend (because the caregivers would go on weekend trips), I never told anyone.

I knew what my being there meant, especially to my mother. On certain weekends during the first winter quarter, I chose to stay on campus. Wright State was very much a commuter's school and thus all but shut down from Friday afternoon to Monday morning. However, I wanted to test my ability to advocate for my own needs. One of the classes at Wright State taught me how to manage my personal care; now was my chance to put theory into practice. I went home for the Thanksgiving/Christmas break during which my mother saw the bruises from my falls and the pressure sores I had developed from being left in the same place all weekend. She was devastated that something like this would happen and frustrated that I didn't tell her, but in her own way understood that I had to spread my proverbial wings.

During winter break I went to Troy High School to visit Brew. I told him everything that had gone on during the first semester of college and he told me that using my voice went both ways. As important as it is to help others, people with disabilities of whatever degree must use their voice and advocate for their own needs. Having a support system is essential and once I got back to school for the winter quarter, I sent many emails home to Brew keeping him abreast of when caregivers weren't showing up to work. I realized how much I counted on his messages of encouragement, inspiring me to keep my chin up and reminding me that nothing in this life worth having is ever easy. No one knows what we need more than we do. Put another way, you and I are our greatest advocates, we have to be willing to speak for ourselves and come to the realization that in the end, no one is accountable for the direction of our lives other than us. It is easy to blame others for our circumstances. I could have, with little effort, held my absent father or my disability responsible for my challenge. The reason I made it through most of the challenges in my life, including the ones at university, is because I knew that the responsibility for the direction of my life was mine alone.

I took an active interest in hiring my own caregivers, beyond the ones that the university chose for me at random. Disability Services provided each of its clients requiring personal care a list of students who applied to be caregivers. I actively interviewed each one and required more of them in terms of punctuality and being thorough in the level of care they were providing. I learned so much in that first year about self-advocacy. The second year I transitioned to care provided by a home healthcare agency; they would come to the dorm as a function of the Ohio Home Care Program under Medicaid. By this time, I understood the necessity to set a higher expectation of the people providing for my basic needs. While there were still difficulties, with caretakers not showing up to work on time (or occasionally at all), I was now equipped to handle it better.

On a particular day when a caregiver was three hours late for the morning shift, I had an 8:00 A.M. science lab with an instructor who had a very strict absence and tardiness policy. For every lab missed, your grade was decreased by one letter, unless you had a justifiable reason. Mindful of my lackluster performance in science courses throughout my education, and realizing that a tardy caretaker may not pass as a worthy excuse, I insisted that the caregiver go with me to the professor's office and explain the situation, complete with the time sheet showing the time of his arrival. After the meeting, the somewhat surprised instructor told me it took guts to make my personal assistant do that. He was so impressed he decided to excuse me from the lab.

In my mind, having guts didn't enter into the equation so much as the new philosophy I had adopted. I was beginning to see that embracing the grind meant more than just accepting life's challenges and advocating on my own behalf; part of it has to do with having a willingness to have difficult or uneasy conversations. Remember the part where I said my advice is hard to follow sometimes, even for me? This is one of those. I avoid confrontation like the Bubonic Plague and I am the last person, of anyone who knows me, that would be described as assertive. However, the more I hear our society speak of safe spaces, and how easily offended we have become, the more I understand that young people have to be taught early that it is okay to disagree, and it is healthy when dealing with other people to openly discuss when they have hurt you or not performed to the best of their ability. I'm not saying that we should be mean, rude, or malicious about it, but we *must* be able and willing to have difficult conversations when they are necessary. This seems so contradictory to the world in which we live, where the fear of offending someone overtakes the need to do what is right. I totally get that it can be a challenge to stand up for oneself, this was especially true for me when it came to my caregivers. When someone has control over how your most personal needs are met, and things go wrong, it can be intimidating to discuss it with them. There is a way of handling confrontation in a professional, non-judgmental, peaceful, yet assertive way. Taking emotion and finger pointing out of the way allows there to, hopefully, be no hurt feelings, yet a deeper understanding and awareness of one's basic needs. No matter what situation you find yourself in, it is essential to remember that correction is a form of caring.

When dealing with my caregivers at university, I always tried to turn problems into teachable moments they could use to improve the way they care for others. This should translate to other areas of life. I've always appreciated correction; I look at it as an opportunity for personal growth. It's easy for someone to praise you for a job well done, but it takes real courage and love to know someone well enough to tell them that they missed the mark. Educators, in many cases, provide the only structure that students have, and as such, they should never be afraid to have difficult conversations with their students. It is in those moments that we become the people we are meant to be and learn those ideals that make us who we are.

College, too, can be an experience where many young people grow and develop who they are as individuals. This was certainly true for me because while the care situation was challenging, and did on more than one occasion cause me to think that there must be an easier way to get an education, it taught me how to speak on my own behalf, and that I could manage my own needs somewhat independent of my mother. University was also the opportunity for me to see how my two passions of government and helping others came together. I had a leg up on many of the other students in the Urban Affairs program because of the mentorship programs in junior high and high school in which I was active and, perhaps, most importantly, the internships I completed during the summers of my college career with the City of Troy.

Each summer during college, I interned with the City of Troy working on research and other projects with the various departments. These experiences each year gave me a backstage pass of sorts to the City that by this time, I had fallen in love with. I found government fascinating, but was more intrigued by how people are impacted on a daily basis by the functions of a municipality. I worked under the City's Assistant Director, Tom Funderburg, who I had met as a high school student during my mentorship with the Mayor. It was from Tom that I gained the exposure and the contacts which enabled me to discern that local government was the profession in which I wanted to pursue. I suppose that I was fortunate in the sense that I began to understand the role city government plays in the lives of the people it serves in practice before theory. So many students do it in the reverse order, whereby the theory comes before any real world applications. I took the projects that I was a part of and used them for research papers and assignments once I was accepted into the Urban Affairs program.

The challenges I faced, particularly with personal assistants, seemed to lessen in the latter two years than my first couple years in college. While I attribute this to my taking an active role in advocating for my own needs, I also think it had something to do with the fact that my focus had shifted somewhat to a course of study about which I was extremely passionate, and in its own way provided a vehicle through which I could be a small influence of good. My junior and senior years of college were reminiscent of my years at Troy High School in the sense that the instructors valued my intellect and judged me on those merits and were less concerned with my physical challenges. My professors in the Urban Affairs department encouraged me to use my experiences at the City of Troy in my writing and activities in college.

April 27, 2013, was the day that many (at least in my early years) never thought would come to pass, college graduation day. It was an unbelievable experience for me, as if the entire day was moving in slow motion. My mother was beside herself with pride as we drove to the Nutter Center Arena next to the university. Beyond crossing the stage when my name was called to receive my diploma, I don't remember much of the two-hour commencement. Instead, images and people of the previous nine years kept forming in my mind. I thought of my mother and how this had to not only be a moment of pride for her, but also a validation of all her dedication. I thought of the events of the last nine years and how, at this particular moment, I was sitting on the edge of a proverbial precipice, at a decision point. Everything we do in our life is a reflection of the people around us and I was acutely aware of all the opportunities that had come my way and the immense responsibility brought with them. Now was the time to give something back to those people and institutions that had given so much to me.

LESSON 5

Accepting Your Mission

One of the many bonds Brew and I share is a mutual admiration of the well-known British Prime Minister Winston Churchill. I used a quote from him in one of the last speeches I gave as a student at Troy High School, which captures one of my philosophies of living. It says, "There comes a certain moment in everyone's life, a moment for which that person was born. That special opportunity, when he seizes it, will fulfill his mission—a mission for which he is uniquely qualified. In that moment, he finds greatness. It is his finest hour." When I graduated college in April of 2013, I knew that my mission was to use what gifts I had been given to be of use to other people.

After three years as a summer intern with the City of Troy, I was fortunate to receive a part time position there working on special projects like the ones I had completed during the internships. I was able to put my B.A. degree in Urban Affairs to good use and earn my very own paycheck. Over time, the position in which I started has evolved into one where I now work primarily with citizens who have questions or comments about City issues and regulations. Talking and helping people are the two areas in which I am most passionate. I am fortunate because my job allows me to blend these two attributes. My role with the City, and the other initiatives in which I am involved, allow me to live my passion. I have learned that true happiness comes from doing what you love and I have often heard it said that if you do what you love, you will never do a day's work in your life. That is why finding what drives you to get up in the morning and nurturing your talent is so important. Everyone has at least one skill that only they can do. When you find that talent, don't be surprised by it, don't try to run from it or excuse it away, instead embrace it and seek people in your life that will uplift you and foster your gifts. Following that formula is what gave me my career and all the other opportunities that came with it.

During the latter part of my college career, I was contacted by Tom Dunn, who by this time was the Superintendent of the Miami County Educational Service Center. The MCESC provides special education resources to the school district within the county. He asked me if I would be willing to speak to his staff about my experiences in Florida - being placed in a special classroom for children with disabilities, how Todd's attitudes left an impact, the sacrifices of not only my mother, but also the men who saw me for my abilities, not my disabilities. It is amazing to think of how some things can take on a life of their own. Out of that one talk came the invitation to give other talks like it. The presentations I gave to educators and students began to spread like a wildfire. Educators who liked the message called Mr. Dunn to book me for their opening staff meetings or teacher in-service trainings.

To this day, a part of me finds it strange, almost wrong, that so many people have been so inspired by my talk because, though I augment it with the lessons that I have learned, the talk is essentially a biographical sketch of at least part of my life. In my mind, there are so many others whose experiences are far more impactful than my own. I realize that we have to use the gifts we are blessed with to better our corner of the world. Each time I am in front of an audience of teachers, I want them to realize that they have the power to save lives every day. While their ability to make a difference may not be as obvious as that of doctor or an emergency medical worker, it is nonetheless just as vital. Many people have asked where I would be today had it not been for Brew and the other people you have read about up to this point. The answer is simple - the speeches, the accolades, my career, and everything that came with it, would not have happened had I not allowed these amazing teachers to impart their wisdom into my life.

My greatest enjoyment is found when I get to speak to students. If the teachers see themselves when I talk about how an educator brought out the best in me, then I see myself in the kids to whom I present. I see the kids from single parent homes, who, like me, are left broken by the absence of a parent who was supposed to love them unconditionally. I like talking to kids because most of them don't have many inhibitions when it comes to asking questions and can spot a fake from a mile away. I can always tell what goes over well with them and what does not. Young people approach me after the talks and they will share their own personal stories with me, stories of how their father left their mother to raise them and their siblings alone. I hear about how parents have to work multiple jobs to support their families. The hardest stories to hear come from kids whose families have substance abuse issues or are abusive to them.   For these students to share their innermost experiences and thoughts with me isn't something I take lightly or casually. It makes me realize that all of the challenges that I faced have been worth it because if something I say can help a student understand that they too have value in themselves and can use the skills they have to better their lives and the other people they come in contact with, I want them to know that in spite of what difficulties they face, at their core, people are genuinely good, and they have to seek out people who will guide them on the right path.

I think students can identify with the lessons I share with them that I learned from Brew and the way that he and the other guys in Troy Schools made me believe in myself. Teachers are one of the most valuable influences on the lives of their students. Alongside parents and families, teachers spend the most time with our young people, and carry a great degree of influence. When I tell the students about my experiences, I want them to realize that there are people in their midst who can have the same impact on them as the special people in my life had on me. As I say in most of my speeches, a teacher's door is always open to making a difference, they are just waiting to be asked.

When the talks to educators and students first started I was pleased that they were well received, albeit surprised. I thought my discussion points about the importance of education, the pivotal role that educators play in a student's development, and the fact that we should never project our preconceived notions on anyone; all of these things I thought were based in common sense and certainly nothing that anyone would consider the makings of a speech that would elicit the kind of emotional response that the ones that I have given have done. Gene Steinke told me that the appeal of the message comes at least in part from the fact that although the truths I speak of are basic, very few people who have been in positions similar to mine are giving credit to the educators who supported them, telling young people that no matter what they face, ultimately they are the arbiters of their own success and there is no justification for anything less. My message must seem so contradictory in a culture which encourages people to avoid discomfort and makes excuses, but it is necessary for our young people to learn the true meaning of resilience and maintaining a strong character.

For as positive as the messages were, and are still, when Tom Dunn began taking me around to various school districts to give talks, I realized that my words had power, but in order for the momentum to continue, I knew that I had to dedicate my time to supporting the youth in my own community. The talks in themselves have value. With each one I want teachers to be empowered to make a difference in the lives of the children they serve and to remember that in spite of all the standardized testing and meaningless red tape which surrounds education, they are an integral catalyst for our youth and their futures. The presentations are in many cases a friendly reminder to educators why it is they do what they do. In that respect, the speeches serve their purpose. For young people, however, I am very cognizant of the fact that it might seem to some of them that it is easy for me to talk to them from the proverbial ivory tower and tell them to try their best and persevere in order to overcome their current realities, some of which may be far more unfortunate than my own. Young people model acts and behavior more than they listen and take heed to an adult's words or positive sentiments. As a teenager who wasn't very street smart, I looked to my own teachers, not so much for the things they said (although that was important), but because they practiced everything they preached.

My presentations to school districts throughout the state of Ohio has given me a platform to do something meaningful for people who need it, and are an essential part of *my* mission. I soon came to the conclusion, however, that talking was only one facet of a much larger picture. If what I was talking about was to be taken seriously, I had to put action behind the words. I wanted to make sure that the opportunities I was given were safeguarded for the students in the future. In addition to my job with the City, I took on a number of board positions with nonprofit organizations with the mission of providing support to the youth within the Troy community.

In September of 2014, I was asked to be on the board of an organization which means a great deal to me. *The Future Begins Today* is a nonprofit organization in Troy with the mission of providing nurturing, mentoring, and scholarship support to Troy students. The kids we serve share a great deal with the ones I speak to - ones like me, who need a hand up in life. November of that year saw the opportunity to bring my presentation to a much wider audience. The Ohio School Boards Association (OSBA) holds an annual conference in Columbus and I was asked to be a presenter for one their breakout sessions. This was a chance to bring my message to a much wider audience with administrators and school officials from all across the state. I wanted this talk in particular to resonate; my mother gave me the best advice as she told me that this was a chance to help bring about real change for Ohio's youth.

Mom said that I should keep talking about Brew and the people that impacted my life as a student because, to use her phrase, "this is no time to preach to the choir." Roughly translated, she meant that this talk shouldn't focus so much on the value of education as my other speeches had done, because everyone there understands the importance of education or they wouldn't be there. She contended that I needed to keep talking about people and put the human face on education. When I got there and gave the talk to roughly 100 school administrators from different districts throughout Ohio, I found that, as usual, Mom was right. So many of them came up to me after the talk and said they couldn't wait to share the story with the teachers in their home districts. This was probably the first time that I truly felt that these talks, as imperfect as they are, might have done some good. The Ohio School Boards Association Conference marked a very important decision point for me.

It began rather casually during the question and answer period at the OSBA presentation. A member of the audience asked if I had any aspirations of public office, given my penchant for public speaking. The Q&A portion of the speeches are always my favorite because I never know what people will ask, especially the kids. I have to confess that not even I was prepared for this question. The people closest to me have long thought being in public office was certainly in my future. I have always believed public service was the highest calling that one could have, and though I find the political process fascinating, I am weary of politicians at all levels of government who forget to check their egos at the door and remember their oath to serve others. Before I knew it, I said that I wanted to run for a position on the Troy City Schools Board of Education. It was a thought that I had been harboring in my mind for some time, but never vocalized to anyone.

After the talk, several people came up to me and told me that I would make a worthy asset to the Board of Education given my experience and view of education. On the ride home, my thoughts were consumed with the idea of running for the school board. I couldn't believe that I actually said it out loud. There is something about verbalizing a long held goal or desire that makes it become more real. Then true to form, doubts immediately assailed me - ones like, how could a soon-to-be twenty- five-year old recent college graduate run a successful campaign? I spoke to my mother about it and as ever she was beyond excited that I would want to try to be of service on our school's Board of Education. The only question she asked was how I arrived at this decision. I told her that moving me to Ohio was the best choice *she* ever made because Troy Schools gave me such a great start and brought a great group of mentors into my life. I wanted to serve as an example to students that people genuinely care about their well-being and have a vested interest in the development of their futures. I also felt that I owed a huge debt of gratitude to Brew for helping my mother raise me, to Chris and Gene for looking after me that first year, and to all the other teachers, like Evil, who put their time into me. Being on the School Board was a definitive way I could say thank you to them, to show my support for them as a board member (votes willing), and allow the teachers in the Troy School system to continue to do what they do best and that is to change students' lives.

Along with her support, I knew that I needed Brew's blessing. After all, it was from him that I learned how to be a man and how to live in service to others. My campaign was a tribute to him. On a visit to Troy High School in the spring of 2015, I visited him in his classroom and asked the all-important question. I hoped I would fare better than I did nine years previously when, as a high school student, I wanted his permission to get my driver's license. This is where my mother appreciated having a male role model for me. Like most parents who don't want to admit to being the overprotective one, when I asked Mother about getting an adaptive license, instead of coming right out and giving her unvarnished point of view, she suggested that I seek Brew's opinion. She figured that would be a win win; I would be getting the opinion of a man that I respected more than any other and who looked out for my best interest, just as much as she did. This plan backfired on me. When I talked to him about it after school one day, his response was an emphatic "NO," to my mom's relief. Looking back, I realize that having my wheelchair parked on his foot during the conversation didn't work in my favor.

Almost a decade later, I still needed the support of the man who gave so much of himself to who I am. This time, however, I had a plan of what I was going to say. Thankfully, when I told Brew of my intention to run for a seat on the School Board as a token of my gratitude to him, Chris, Gene, Evil and the teachers of our district who help kids every day, with a smile on his face, he said, "If that is what you really want to do, I want it too." That in my mind is the best definition of love; wanting for someone you care about the same thing that they do. With Brew's support came one of those life lessons that I have counted on at so many points during my life.

He cautioned me that an effective elected official does not always follow the majority and isn't anyone's puppet or mouthpiece, but is rather someone that has the ability to think for themselves and do what is right over what is expected. It is so easy to go along with what the crowd or group is doing, but it takes a strong individual who is willing to take the difficult path and ask the hard questions. We are so quick to take everything at face value, but those who have the greatest impact never cease to ask questions and do the homework necessary to make sound decisions. Brew's support made me feel as though I was ready to embark on the next phase of my mission.

In June of 2015, an article appeared in the local newspaper about the resignation of one of the school board members. It went on to read that the Board would be accepting letters of interest from anyone wishing to be considered to fill the unexpired term. Luckily, I had been attending board meetings fairly regularly since OSBA and had heard this specific vacancy would be coming. So I had my letter ready to go on the day after the request for candidates was made public. Too important to leave to the mail, I hand delivered my letter to the Board of Education.

A couple of days after dropping off the letter, I received a call from the Superintendent of Troy Schools to say that the board had received five applicants for consideration and asked if I would come in for an interview at 4:30 that Thursday afternoon. I readily agreed. Panic set in after I saw there were a total of five candidates who were applying for the seat. I wasn't necessarily afraid of competition, my years spent on speech teams gave me the ability to put obstacles like that in perspective. What made me uneasy were the caliber of people which had applied, a wet-behind the ears recent college graduate didn't stack up well (in my mind) against a lawyer, a financial manager, and two local businessmen. I never wanted to backslide so much in my life as I did when I read those names in the paper, the majority of whom I knew and respected. I got no sympathy from my mother, who in addition to being my full time caregiver, never tired of giving me a taste of my own medicine. She reminded me why I was embarking on this journey: to give something back to the district that gave so much to me. "Besides," she cautioned, "Mr. Brewer and the guys didn't teach you to run away when things get difficult. Doing that would be a slap in the face to them."

Wishing to avoid that ignoble end, I decided to proceed with the interview. I told the board of my vested interest in the district and my desire to move it forward and about how the speeches I had given to school districts and OSBA strengthened my resolve to make a positive change for the young people in our district. The board seemed very receptive to my point of view and while they didn't select me to fill the unexpired term (very wisely they chose someone with previous school board experience who was very adept at understanding finance), the School Board President called me and proffered the hope that I would take out a petition and run in the election the next fall.

I gave that serious consideration and talked it over with Tom Funderburg at the City. He is another great source of advice and good counsel for me. He is one of those people that allow you to feel good just by being in his presence and has been a monumental support to me professionally and in helping find how my strengths would best be of use to serve my community. He showed me how to cultivate an image that I wanted to project - someone who was ready, willing, and able to make a difference through community service. Each one of us has to make a choice about what image we want to portray to the wider world. Tom said that if I was really serious about running, I needed to show my commitment and keep going to board meetings and other school events. Tom said that would show my dedication to the district and keep me abreast of issues facing the schools.

The first step of any campaign for public office is taking out petitions of registered voters.   Board of Education candidates in the county where I live are required to get 75 signatures of residents throughout the district. I was fortunate to get 150. Then came the task of campaigning. As I began that August of 2015, I knew there would be four people running for three open seats. I printed campaign brochures, made yard signs, and asked well known community members to submit letters of support to the local newspaper. I was never more nervous than I was in the days after I took out the petitions. All the talking and preparation in the world didn't assail my nerves about how I was going to beat an incumbent on the school board. Even though there was a sort of acclaim which accompanied my speeches, certainly the national one, I was still relatively unknown in Troy, Ohio.

One weekend in late August of 2015, I was preparing a list of talking points about my goals for the school district and trying to find ways of "selling myself" (to borrow my mother's phrase), when I read an article in the online edition of the *Troy Daily News*, which said that the Miami County Board of Elections held a meeting the previous night to certify all the petitions submitted by potential candidates for all the races held on November 3, 2015. They went on to say all the petitions were filled out correctly and the signatures on them were in fact valid ones of registered voters. I was puzzled as I went down the long list of those which were accepted for elections within the entire county, my name was one of three which were "validated" for the Troy City Schools Board of Education; there were four of us running for three seats. My mind was running as I scanned the list of petitions that were "denied" by the Board of Elections for invalid signatures or incorrect dates on the petitions. My eyes darted to a familiar name, the fourth candidate had his petition denied by the Board. Like someone putting the pieces of the puzzle together, I tried to think about what this meant for my own campaign.

From my work in local government, I knew that while he could still run as a write-in candidate, my efforts were just made much easier. In a burst of excitement, I jostled my mother from her nap to share the exciting news. She shared in the joy of the moment, but asked a very apropos question, "What happens now?" I knew that the job of campaigning may have lessened by the traditional standards, yet I couldn't afford to be complacent. I still wanted the people of our district to know who it was that would, in all probability, be representing them and the students in our schools. I went ahead with the letter writing initiative. As odd as this may seem for a surely uncontested election, I wanted these well respected people in Troy to introduce me to the public; it was important for me to know that people knew what they were getting by voting for me. Letters which appeared in the newspaper and online from retired educators and community leaders spoke for me and not only laid out my qualifications and desire to serve, but associated my name with the Troy Board of Education.

In the days after, the article about the petitions appeared. I have to confess, I was overtaken with a mild case of Obsessive Compulsive Disorder. While I understood that it was quite likely that I was a shoo-in for the November election, and indeed the seat in January, I knew that I could leave no stone unturned. I instructed my mother to call the Board of Elections every day for the week leading up to the cut off day for the submission of write-in candidates to see if the candidate whose petitions were rejected chose to run as a write-in. She wanted to do everything she could to help me because she knew how much serving on the Board meant to me; she was concerned, however, that officials at the Board of Elections would recognize her voice if she called each day for a week. I told her not to worry, anyone from the public can call and ask for a listing of candidates for any election, but if she was really concerned, she could always disguise her voice (she was a fabulous mimic). I don't know if she ever used an impression; I *do* know that her calls yielded the desired result: no one ran as a write-in and the seat was mine.

In the run-up to election day, I kept attending board meetings and familiarizing myself with school issues so I could hit the ground running. November 3, 2015, was Election Day. I only needed one vote, but the final tally showed that I received 4,788! It made me smile to think that my mother's, Brew's, and the others were amongst the votes in my favor, electing me to serve not only the students in our community, but also the teachers I respect and admire so much. The best part of success is making those you love proud of you. January 11, 2016, was a point of pride for me, my mother and all those who got me to that point; it was the day I was sworn in as a member of the Troy City Schools Board of Education. I was so pleased that I was in a position where I could do some good for a district that brought so much positivity to my own life. I was equally thrilled that my mother was there to see me take the oath of office and my first official meeting as a board member.

On the way to the meeting, Mom said she was probably more proud of me on that day than at any other point in my life. I thought for certain that college graduation would have trumped everything before and after it in her mind. But she said that this was the one she was proudest of because anyone can get noticed for doing something well like writing or speaking. "Remember," she said, "when you sit behind that desk you aren't just representing everyone who ever believed in you, but you are a mouthpiece of the ideals that Mr. Brewer taught you. Be true to those and you can't miss," she smiled.

Taking the oath was a surreal moment. I couldn't escape the juxtaposition of being that kid in the multi-handicapped classroom, who few people thought would ever be able to write his own name, to a nationally recognized public speaker to now a college graduate holding public office before the age of thirty. As I swore to support the Constitution of the United States and to "faithfully and impartially discharge my duties as a member of the Troy

City School Board of Education," I knew that none of it would have been possible were it not for the sacrifices of the woman sitting in the back of the room.

During the meeting, the President of the board acknowledged Mother and after a brief moment of panic (she got that deer in headlights look) she nodded with a smile. After the meeting, she was asked her thoughts on her son becoming a board member and where she found the fortitude to raise me all alone and still be my sole caregiver. She replied, "That's just it, I didn't do it alone. Michael is doing this as a thank you to Mr. Brewer and those other wonderful men who took him under their wings. All I did," she said, "was chauffeur him where he needed to go. Taking care of him is my job as his parent." She believed that was *her* mission - but mine could not have begun without her. If through my role as a school board member I can remind teachers of the power they have to change lives, or I can inspire one student to find their passion and the people that can help them nurture it, then that is my responsibility, and one that I am very proud of. There is a quote from famed baseball player Roberto Clemente that I really like. Clemente says, "Any time you have the opportunity to make a difference in the world and you don't, then you are wasting your time on Earth." To me, these words encapsulate the mission of life which is in truth, very simple - to be the good in the world.

Well in to 2016, I felt like I was really making a difference in the life of my community. I loved my job, I was thrilled to be on the school board, and was fortunate enough to volunteer with a number of organizations within Troy, each of which had a very positive impact on the people they serve. In 2015, I was even named the Outstanding

Young Man of the Year by the Troy Area Chamber of Commerce. This honor, and its female counterpart, is given to men and women under the age of 40 who have made significant contributions to their community. This was an incredible honor. But it's important to put awards like this into perspective. It is wonderful to be praised for a job well done and we wouldn't be human if we didn't feel proud at moments like these. But we should never lose sight of our why. Put another way, awards and praise should never be what motivates us to make a difference. I have been blessed with many moments of achievements in my life and am grateful for each and every one of them. But I would honestly give them all back tomorrow as long as I could still have Brew and the inner circle in my life, and the opportunity to do good for another person.

I asked my mom one day that with all the wonderful things and people that have come into my life, if she had any regrets about anything. She talked about how she didn't regret anything and was very proud of everything that I had accomplished, but her concern was that if anything were to happen to her, that I would not be left alone. It had been just the two of us (in terms of family) since my grandfather passed away in 2012. Though she was never one to talk about her struggles and maintained a perpetual stiff upper lip, it had to be unimaginable for her that she not only lost a parent, but the one person in her family, who supported her choice to raise me over placing me in an institution.

I'm sure she thought that she would have other children, but Todd's early departure complicated things to such an extent that I think she was worried about survival and that anything beyond my own success and welfare was secondary to her wants and desires. She used to say that I needed to surround myself with a strong inner circle who would be a surrogate family of sorts and provide a support system so that I would never be alone. I couldn't ever bring myself to think about a time when my mother wouldn't be around. There are some people whose lives are so integral to our own that it seems inconceivable that they would one day be gone. I would soon know exactly how that would feel and learn one of the most important life lessons to date.

LESSON 6

The Definition of Family

After graduation from college, my mother once again assumed the role of the lone caregiver for me. I was glad she got a bit of respite while I was in college (except when I was home on weekends), but here she was again ready to sacrifice her life so that I could have one. The care provided to me while in college was provided for the most part by homecare agencies and paid for by the state. For whatever reason, the area where I lived was very difficult to staff with caregivers through the Ohio Homecare Program. My case manager at the time indicated that there was a provision whereby my mother could be employed by a care agency and thus be compensated for seeing to my personal needs.

At first, she was appalled at the idea of getting paid for that which she saw as her calling. I pointed out to her that under normal circumstances, I would be out on my own and supporting myself, but this was a way that I could give something back to her for the dedication she was giving me. I don't think she bought that argument for a moment, but she agreed to it anyway, primarily because she didn't want me to lose the Medicaid benefits, which would provide for my personal care when she was no longer able. Mom was a forward thinker, a planner who seemed to be one step ahead. Two years after I graduated from college, I noticed that Mom was slowing down. She was still able to care for me, but I couldn't help but notice that her stamina just wasn't what it once had been and she was talking more and more about what would happen to me if she weren't around.

She never liked to focus on herself. Growing up I don't ever remember her going to the doctor or doing really anything for herself. Looking back, I think she was so concerned about making sure that I was taken care of, and had all the tools I needed to be successful, that she put her needs aside. It took some persuasion to actually get her to see a physician and get to the bottom of why she was feeling so badly. Blood tests found that she was suffering from an autoimmune disease, causing a hardening of her organs. In true Patricia Ham fashion, however, she categorically refused to allow this "minor setback" from detouring her from caring for me. She even went so far as to reschedule a procedure to install an intravenous port in her chest which would deliver medicine to her heart so I wouldn't miss a school board meeting!

In thinking about the level of devotion my mother showed to me, I appreciate how fortunate I was to have her. From an early age, she taught me that taking care of me was her duty. I realize, though, that she didn't necessarily have to make that choice. She could have very easily agreed to Todd's ultimatum to institutionalize me when I was young, or at any point decided that it was all too much and that she didn't sign on to be a nurse. Quitting, however, wasn't in her repertoire.   Mom's oft repeated expression was that she was going to take care of me until the day she died.

Everyone has days which mark a steep change in their lives. I certainly have had many of those and January 5, 2017, was another. My abiding memory of the day my mother died was the ordinariness of how it started. We went through the usual morning routine. She bathed and dressed me, making sure I had everything I needed for the day. Mom and I talked about the day ahead and a presentation I had scheduled for the following week. As I left I told her, "I will see you later, I love you."

She was gone when I came home that afternoon. I found her lying face down on the floor by her desk and at first I thought she had passed out. I called out to her twice with no response.   I immediately called the paramedics. Upon arrival, they sent me immediately out of the house. I think because some of them knew who I was through working at the City, the first responders wanted to be sure that my last memory of my mother was not this. As I sat outside on that cold January afternoon, my mind was a mixture of emotions. Shock, sadness, fear, but overall the most colossal sense of disbelieving numbness. "What am I to do now?" is the question that kept repeating itself perpetually in my mind.   I couldn't understand how this happened. I knew she had the autoimmune disease, but I didn't anticipate anything like this. One of the paramedics stopped my cascade of thoughts and emotions when he very quietly uttered the words that no son ever wants to hear, "she has passed away." It was as if I had entered some sort of parallel universe or some awful nightmare from which there was no waking up. The official cause of her death was a heart attack. Mercifully, the paramedics, knowing that I was employed by the City of Troy, called Tom Funderburg and his assistant, Julie, whom I have been close to since job shadowing the mayor at the age of fourteen. She shared my mother's kindness and, along with Brew, edited a number of the speeches I gave in high school.

It was decided that I would stay at the fire station that night while caregivers were established and while the funeral was being planned. Everyone was immensely kind and attended to my every need. The enormity of what had happened laid heavy on me the whole night long. I couldn't reconcile the fact that this woman which had been so essential to my daily living and a driving force behind my success, was gone in an instant. I didn't know what was coming next; I had lived a very sheltered life up to that point in terms of being "street smart." While I had my own checking account and credit cards, my exposure to finance ended with me giving my mother a check each month for my half of the expenses. Now, I had a house that was totally outfitted for my needs, which I owned, and all of the responsibilities which come with it.

In the days following Mom's passing it felt as though I couldn't really grieve for her because there was so much to learn about living on my own. That whatever sadness I felt that she was gone must be put aside so that I could learn all that I didn't know. I think, too, that the shock of what happened made me numb. When one loses the only family they have, you also forego a piece of yourself, and as such, you treasure people with whom you share a common history and who know you well. In the last days of her life, my mother talked a lot about how grateful she was for Brew, Chris, Gene, Evil and the other people and opportunities which had come my way. She told me two days before she passed that should anything happen to her, she hoped I would reach out to Brew because he would look after me. She also said to form my own inner circle and create a surrogate family. She went on to say that should she have to leave me, she would send a stand-in for her to take her space. Mom wanted a parental figure to keep me out of trouble. Upon reflection, I believe these pieces of advice and the retrospective mood was her ever so subtle way of telling me time was short, almost as if this was her way of saying goodbye.

One of the first people to reach out to me hours after Mom's passing was Natalie Rohlfs, the Executive Director of *The Future Begins Today*, in which I was, at the time, and currently am, a board member. Natalie has one of the sweetest dispositions of anyone I have ever met. She speaks cogently, yet softly. Hearing her voice allowed me to feel somewhat at peace. My mother loved Natalie and I had become close with her in the year since she took over the organization. She contacted Brew, who was exactly the person I had been wanting and needing to see. I didn't know how or when, but somehow, I knew he was going to be the one that would make sense of the world again.

Like he had done so many times before, Brew called and somehow made me believe for an instant that everything was going to be all right in my world again. When he called me the morning after Mom's death, for the first time in about eighteen hours I felt that I could actually breathe. He made arrangements to see me when I returned home from staying at the fire station. So many people were surrounding me at that time and I cannot describe how their immense kindness eased the burden of that early shock. I needed Brew, my frother, because I share a bond with him that is unlike any others in my life. It is odd how even now I don't have to say anything at all, yet he somehow knows the thoughts in my head before I think them. We all have someone like that in our lives and if ever I needed his support, it was in that moment. Brew went out of his way to make sure that I had the support I needed. He met with caregivers and like he is still today, was on hand to give advice to my never ending questions. He knows me better than anyone in my life and in that moment, was able to reach me in a way that no one else could.

In addition to my mother and late grandfather, Brew had been my only "family" in the sense that he filled so many roles in my life. Somehow he managed to brilliantly combine the roles of father, brother, confidant, and best friend. Five months after Mom passed, he expanded my definition of family in a very special way. Brew took me to his mother's horse farm five minutes from where I live. To know Clarice Francis is to love her because of the love and kindness she radiates. You know how it is when you meet someone and you have an instant connection? That's how I felt when I met her. I owe her so much because without her, I wouldn't have met the most important man in my life. She reminded me so much of my own mother. Not only were they the same age (my mom was actually two weeks older than Clarice), but I describe them both as steel cloaked in velvet. They both have the most generous souls on the planet, yet they have an inner strength and grit that fortifies them and makes them very protective of the people they care about. No one can ever replace one's mother; when they are gone there is a void that can never be filled in quite the same way.   No matter how old we get, there is a comfort in knowing that your parents are around.   That feeling becomes all the more prevalent when you've, in reality, lost the only one you have.   I was so lucky to have my mother for 26 years; her sacrifices and unconditional support guided me where I am today.   In death, I believe my mom was rendering one final act of care, sending me an inner circle who redefined my concept of family.

"Mom" isn't a title that I give to just anyone. As you have read, I have been infinitely lucky to have so many people care about me.   But Clarice holds claim to a special place in my heart that few people do.   My relationship with her reminds me every day of   one indelible truth about life.   Namely, that one doesn't have to share biology with someone to love them as their own child.   I call Clarice my second Mom because she fills a gap in my life.   She is the one I go to when I need motherly advice and a shoulder to lean on, the one who I want to tell when something good happens, and the person who can bring me back down to earth on those rare days when life becomes too much. She manages to dull the pain of Mom's loss by being there when I need her the most and being the voice of my mother in the world, giving me that maternal guidance Mom would have given me.   There is something very strange about losing a parent in your twenties, especially when one is as dependent as I was. After all, I *am* grown, and had circumstances been different, I may well have been on my own before mom passed.   But as it is, there are still areas of my life in which I need support and advice.   Everything from dealing with caregivers to the responsibilities of being a homeowner are things that I go to Clarice for. She gladly accepts the mantle of surrogate mother whenever I need her.

The same characteristics that I admire about Brew are equally manifested in his mom. Of all the treasures that he brought to my life since he saved it, I think I will always be most grateful for sharing his own mother with me and to her for loving me as her own child. Some of you reading this know exactly what it's like to be without parents in the traditional sense. I want to encourage you to find that guidance in your life. Never allow the difficult circumstances in your life to close your heart to people who may come into it, especially when there is a hole that needs to be filled. There is one role that Clarice takes on that means the most to me, when she is able, she will accompany me to various presentations I give to schools and other groups, and sit in the back just the way my mother used to do. Knowing that there is someone in the audience who believes in me and takes parental pride in what I do means everything.

When Mom passed I had absolutely no idea what it was like to live on my own. New caregivers came in the day after her passing and in a way it was very odd how swiftly life took on a new normal. Compared to what I thought would happen (I had brief visions of having to go into a care facility and leaving everything that was familiar), Brew was somehow able to keep me grounded and took me into his family. I realize that, in a way, I need him more now than I did as a student. My relationship with him has been one of the greatest blessings in my life and one that comes along once in a lifetime. Of all the titles and positions: national speaking champion, public servant, school board member, author, the one that means the most to me is being considered part of his family.

How does one even begin to repay someone who has always given the best of themselves to you, been there for you at every turn, celebrating your joys and sharing in your difficulty? Every honor and accolade I have earned is due in large part to his belief in me and the time Brew put into mentoring me. Part of my ability to persevere comes from knowing that whatever happens, he'll always be in my corner. After Mom died, I was sorting through some of her belongings when I came across the national gold medal I won in Orlando. The medal symbolized a great achievement for me and marked just how far I had come, as well as, the dedication that Brew had to my success. I knew that medal ultimately belonged to him. I took the award, which is the only one of its kind in the area, and had it engraved with his name and a message on the back, thanking him for all the support he had given me. He loved it and mentioned in passing that he would like to have a hard case in which to permanently display it. For his birthday the following year, I asked Evil to sneak into Brew's classroom and get it so that I could have it framed. I grossly underestimated the value that Brew placed on the medal; I had it removed on a day that as luck would have it, he was out sick from school. I figured he wouldn't notice it was gone. I was wrong, very wrong. Thinking that it was one of his students playing a prank, he offered bonus points to anyone with information leading to its safe return, even going so far as to look into buying a medal to replace it. He scoured the internet trying to find an exact replica of the medal and racked his brain to remember the inscription on the back, in hopes that he could quickly replace it so I wouldn't notice its absence. He could not, for the life of him, find a replica to replace my national finalist medal! He didn't know what to do. He didn't know where the medal had gone and he didn't know who took it or how he would ever replace it or get it back. This would explain the look of relief on his face when he unwrapped the medal, complete with a display case, on his birthday. It may be something small in the grand scheme of life, but that medal represents an accomplishment that was mine, but would not have been conceived or possible were it not for Brew's guidance.

Each one of us need an inner circle, people who become a surrogate family of sorts. There is a well-known adage that says, "you can pick your friends, but not your family." That is certainly true. When Mom passed away, for all intents and purposes, the family unit that I knew, came to the most abrupt end. Having Brew there to make everything all right, just as he had done so many times in the past, got me through those impossibly difficult days.

There is a comfort in having people who have known you for a significant portion of your life swoop in to support you, when you no longer have the one person who has been with you since the day you were brought into the world. One of the first people to reach out to me after Mom died was Chris. The person who had a front row seat to the beginning of this remarkable journey reassured me that just as he did many years previously, he would look after me when I needed him. Knowing that gave me strength. I share a bond with Chris that has lasted. Chris reminded me how to laugh again, like he did with the young man in a new hometown. He reminded me that joy can be found in the middle of the worst times that life has to offer.

Chris' constant question to me is "Are you good?" Like Brew and the others in my "inner circle," Chris goes out of his way to make sure that I have what I need. As if time has stood still, Chris often goes into full scale caretaker mode and makes sure that I want for nothing. His family also means a great deal to me; he is the only boy in a family of three girls. His sisters are extremely special to me and bring me so much happiness. Being an only child has allowed me to appreciate the chaos and activity that comes with large families.

My job with the City, and role on the Board of Education, carried me through the first few months of life on my own. This, coupled with my other community involvement and presentations, gives me a sense of purpose and direction. Life changes so swiftly and our ability to adapt to it can surprise us at times. I learned a lot about myself after my mother passed away. For as many times as I have spoken in public about the value of overcoming obstacles, there were brief moments where I wondered how it was I could survive without the woman who devoted her life to me.

Thanks to Brew, Chris, Gene, Evil and those who are in the unenviable position of knowing the real me, I'm making it with a new definition of the word family, as well as a little help from a recent addition to the band of brothers I have formed. Every person who comes in to our lives has something to teach us. Up to this point, it is evident how the people in my life have left their own unique impression, both good and bad. Think about the people in your life who are the most important to you. What is it that they bring to your life? Have you ever had someone have your back like Chris does mine? Possibly a mentor like Gene who makes you smile and inspires you to achieve things you never thought possible, or Evil who challenges your thought process and makes you think about ideas in different ways. Maybe you have a teacher or coach in your life who knows you better than most and means more to you than anyone else, like Brew does to me. You might have a devoted parent like my mother who makes many sacrifices on your behalf. If you are truly blessed, you may also have a second mother like Clarice who lets you adopt her and loves you like you are her own.

It is important to thank whomever makes your life worth living for the role they have in your life. There is something very special about people who know and love you for the person you are, not what they want you to be. Hold fast to these people because they will be the ones who you can count on no matter what. Every once in a while it is necessary to expand your inner circle. I did so after Mom died and in doing so found someone who inspires me every day.

Natalie Rohlfs was such an immense help to me after Mom passed away and she recruited her husband, Brad, to take me to church each Sunday. I had known Brad indirectly as a football coach with Brew, Chris, Gene, and Evil. I really got to know him after Natalie took over as Executive Director of *The Future Begins Today*, and was immediately struck by his personality. There are certain people who fill every room they enter with the most awesome energy, that's Brad. I was excited to get to know him better. It is often said if you want to know the true measure of a person, study how they treat other people. When Brad was approached about helping me, he readily agreed to take me to church each Sunday. There was no hesitation, no thinking about it, just a willingness to be there for someone who needs him.

That is the first lesson I learned from Brad. Most people would describe themselves as willing to help others, but how fast do we say yes when the opportunity arises? Brad immediately agreed to step in and help wherever he could. He didn't say, "let me think about it" or asked what was in it for him. This is the attitude everyone should have. We all know the value of giving someone a helping hand, but how quick are we to do it? Do we say yes the way Brad did without any regard to what we might personally gain from the experience or relationship? Giving to others doesn't require grand gestures or vast sums of money, but can be achieved through small acts carried out with great love. The good we do for others should never be governed by self-serving motives, but a genuine desire to represent the good in the world. Each of the people who you have read about and have made a difference in my life, did so not because they wanted anything, quite the opposite. These people are in my life because they genuinely care about me. They never wanted any recognition or praise for it, but did it because they wanted to have a small impact on the life of someone who needed them.

Brad was no different. The ride to church each week was a highlight. These Sunday strolls are where I really got to know the man who is one of my closest confidants. What I find so amazing is that Brad was like the missing piece of the most intricate puzzle. The people who had meant the most to me were about the same age, each one graduating Troy High School within a few years of each other, as football players, and all, at one point or another, football coaches. Brad is also a teacher in Troy. With his background in Special Education, Brad takes a keen interest in students that need extra attention, those which the casual observer might easily dismiss. The kids who are forgotten are the kids Brad takes under his wing. These make the best teachers; the ones who realize that they aren't just mass producing a group of thinkers who can pass standardized tests. Rather, they are helping to shape who they will become for a lifetime. I cannot imagine where I would be had it not been for Brew and the others getting a hold of me when they did. Now Brad was about to do the same. Each time I talked to Brad, I noticed that we had quite a bit in common. I think that if one put me on two good legs, we may very well end up with Brad's identical twin, at least ideologically.

One of the many attributes we share is a positive disposition. Brad is one of the most optimistic people I have ever met, always with a smile on his face. This is the way I have always tried to live. Being positive and finding the good is a decision we make on a daily basis and something we *choose* to do. Good comes from all things if we are willing to seek it out. There have been countless times in my life when that which is positive seems fleeting or impossible to find. But it's there. We cannot afford to take the easy way out. As bad as things seem, nothing lasts forever and there are always reasons to hold on to hope. Think about all you have going for you in your life. As hard as the trials are in our lives, can we honestly say that we have not learned something from them? In examining my own experiences, I note that had I never been placed in the position of having a disability, I might never have found my ability to articulate my thoughts in a way that would resonate with the young people who hear my messages. Equally, had Todd not left my mother and I when I was so young, we might never have moved to Ohio and I would never have had someone like Chris to look after me and introduce me to Brew who erased all the negativity and made me realize that there was something special inside me.

Here, now, was another choice. The temptation to give up was very great, but I think of what I would have missed had I closed myself off to the world and everyone in it. The true definition of family ... is a group of people who care about you no matter what. They come in many different varieties and backgrounds, but share one common trait. Love is the tie that binds people together for an eternity. If you are reading this and lack that familial base in your life, do not despair. We have been given a unique opportunity of choosing the people who make up our family. The bond you share with the people you were born to is sacred and should be treasured, but when you don't have it in its fullness, find people who will lift your soul and love you as you are. They are out there; you just have to be willing to find them.

This is what Brad brings to my life. He is the person to whom I entrust my deepest and innermost feelings about virtually everything. We all need someone in our life who allows us to be ourselves. Brad shares my vision on so many aspects of life such as finding the positive in every circumstance and doing at least one kind act every day to make another person smile. That is why it's easy for me to share my daily life with him. Brad has one of the biggest hearts of anyone I know. Do you have a friend or sibling that you share your closest thoughts with? It's one of the greatest gifts we can have. That is who Brad is to me. His optimism is infectious and the joyful way of life transmits wherever he takes his smile. The happiness Brad exudes is surpassed only by the depth of his desire to bring out the best in other people.

I count myself blessed that he came into my life and filled it with such positivity. Our point of view is shaped by the people we allow around us. The life we have been given is a priceless treasure that we should value above all else. The people we let into it, should enrich it, not deplete it. It didn't take Brad long to enrich *my* life in a very special way. He is the brother that everyone should have, and I'm so honored he's mine, with two ears that listen and an attitude that is free of judgement, but gives an honest opinion when elicited. I think what makes our relationship work so well is that, like the others, he can pretty much say whatever he likes to me, and he does. I count on his frankness; he somehow has the ability to get me to turn off my filter and be myself.

I knew virtually next to nothing about being on my own when Brad and I first got to know one another. Brad made me a part of his family and expanded my support system just when I needed that in my life.

Of all the presentations I give, the ones I enjoy the most are the ones I get to do in my home school district. When I was elected to the school board I felt as though I was vested with a responsibility to help assure that our students have every opportunity possible to be successful. Within a year of joining the Board of Education, I was asked to give a talk to the entire student body. I enjoy talking about those that have impacted me to Troy students because in many cases I'm talking about people they know or teachers they have had themselves.

It was so exciting being in the place where my journey began so many years before. What made it all the more special was that the speech was held on October 16th, Chris' birthday.

I arrived at the school well before speech time and asked if I could go visit the man for whom I was a student aide, Gene. I was so thrilled that he would be in the audience. It was partially because of his nudging that I became a speaker in the first place. Gene gave me so much support my first year in Troy, and was one of the first people to see me instead of my challenges. Gene says that he is happy to be a spoke in the wheel that is my success. In reality he became so much more. As an adult, he is inspiring me still with his zeal for life. It sometimes gets difficult for someone in my position to live independently and assume all the responsibilities that go along with it. Gene is there every day to remind me of my inner strength and the ability that I have to rise above whatever comes my way.

These are the type of people that we should strive to have as part of our lives; people who bring out the best in us and are willing to care about our wellbeing. Life is a testing ground comprised of unimaginable peaks and valleys which can be devastating. The way in which we react to our circumstances determines the direction our future will take. Sure there are challenges, but equally there are opportunities which enable us to rise above our current reality. However, the choices we make have the greatest impact on how our story unfolds. The best choice you can make is to bring people in your life who make up a picture of the ideals you represent. That's family. That's life's richest blessing.

THE FINAL EXAM

A Return to Washington D.C.

You are probably intrigued or puzzled that I chose to write about a trip to our nation's capital to mark the last chapter of this book. I did so because we are visual people, meaning that we need tangible signs that we are achieving our goals and being successful at whatever we are doing. It starts when we are young; we earn grades which are a barometer of how we are comprehending what we have learned. As adults who enter the professional world, we often get reviews or evaluations, which give us an indication of how effectively we are performing our duties. When I was elected to the school board, the fact that I got more than a handful of votes in an uncontested race signified that a significant number of voters felt that I was qualified to fill the role. Signs like these are the greatest indicator that what we are doing is making a difference.

Giving speeches to school districts and other organizations is a role in which I take great pride knowing that each speech, in its own way, is leaving a positive impression on the audiences who hear it. The letters I get from students thanking me for inspiring them and making them realize that they too have the ability to make something special of their lives no matter their circumstances, gives me so much purpose and joy in my life. That is my greatest hope with this book; that one person finds reasons to persevere and live life to the fullest. Each invitation in which I get to speak is proof to me that the story does have meaning to some people. In November of 2017, I took a phone call from a friend who works in the Ohio Treasurer of State's office. He said that his office was asked to find someone to speak about living with a disability on Capitol Hill in Washington D.C. They were also looking for someone who uses a STABLE Account. A STABLE account is made possible by the federal Achieving a Better Life Experience ("Able") Act, which is a savings account, of sorts, into which disabled people can safely place their resources without fear of losing their Medicaid benefits, which brings with them certain requirements with regards to income. My job with the City of Troy made it quite natural for me to have one of those accounts and I was elated about the prospect of speaking in Washington D.C.

My mind went immediately back to the prediction Brew made when I was in high school, that one day my speaking ability would take me there. I knew he had to be there and watch what he envisioned a decade before. Chris had never been to Washington and one thing I take the greatest joy in is making him feel special. He was there when public speaking was merely a thought in my mind, so it was only right that he be there to see one of the defining moments in my quasi-public speaking career.

Knowing that this was going to be a big moment for me, I couldn't let it pass without Brad being part of it. I don't think he could quite process what it was I was telling him on the phone when I called to tell him. He does so much to support me that I had to share it with him. Before I knew it I had the makings of what is commonly known as a "guys trip." There is no other group of people I would have rather shared this experience with.

Arriving in Washington D.C. was an unforgettable experience. There was something vastly different about being there this time than was the case ten years previously. Although the 2008 youth leadership forum was quite an honor, I was one of hundreds of students from across the nation and while I was elected to lead the forum, I did not speak in the actual Capital building. This was the big time. The plan was that I would be part of a panel of legislators and lobbyists who were trying to understand more about the disability community and about STABLE Accounts. I was about to give voice to the issues facing people who are challenged with a disability and the need for programs which allow us to provide for the future.

The morning of the presentation came, it was very harrowing knowing that I would be speaking in the same room within the U.S. Senate building where the Watergate and Teapot Dome hearings were held. This was my chance to play a small part in bringing about real change for those whose lives are impacted by a handicap. I spoke about the challenges I face on a daily basis in terms of care and the activities of daily living and how vitally important it is for someone in my position to plan for the future and how these accounts financially enable me to do that.

As I sat at the end of this long table in the Russell Senate building where so many moments of American History had taken place, I had such a sense of pride, especially toward our great democracy. I felt honored that I was asked to speak in our nation's capital about a topic in which I am fiercely passionate. Herein lies another barometer of success. If you can say at the end of the day that you have done at least one thing to give hope and courage to another person, nothing else matters.

The trip to the nation's capital was a first in more ways than one. This was the first guys trip I had ever taken. I don't think I've ever laughed so much as I did in those two days. This was a new experience for me. It marked the first time I roomed with a group of guys, the first time in almost two decades that I was able to sit in the front of a vehicle (I sit in the back of my personal van where the lift is located). The van we took to Washington had the front passenger seat removed so that a wheelchair could be secured in its place. I was riding shotgun .... and I loved it! This trip was also the first time I tried alcohol. The guys took me to lunch after the presentation in downtown D.C. to celebrate. I tried some of Brad's vodka and tonic water with lime. To me it looked a bit like Sprite or 7UP. I liked the taste; it was very refreshing with a bit of a kick. It is important to be open enough to try new things. That is not to say that we should use having an open mind as excuse to drink! Although I never joined a fraternity in college, this sojourn to the nation's capital gave me an idea of what they are like. This was the first time I shared a room with someone. Even in college I was in a dorm room by myself, here the hotel gave us two rooms;

I roomed with Brew on the trip and I asked him at one point if this adventure had been everything he had imagined it would be when he made the prediction that I would speak in Washington. He said it was better, and it certainly was for me as well.

Being in the cradle of American government was a once in a lifetime experience that will last in my memory for a lifetime. I can't help but think about how my mother would have been so proud and happy that I had this band of brothers around me. I found the family she wanted me to have. The rest of the day after the presentation was spent touring the nation's capital. Washington D.C. might never be the same after they let the four of us in. We were almost asked to leave the Museum of American History by a very imposing security guard after Chris committed the heinous crime of snapping a picture. I got us out of trouble by telling the guard that she was in the presence of the best American History teacher in the country. She said that if he was so great he should well be able to answer three questions about the Constitution. If he answered all three questions correctly, she would let us go. I noted that she didn't say what would happen if he got one wrong. However, in true highly qualified teacher style, Brew came through and answered all three questions correctly. That minor hurdle behind us, a tour of the Capitol building awaited us. Brad has a high school friend who works in security for the Capitol building and arranged a tour. It was absolutely overwhelming to be at the epicenter of the American Legislative process. Every inch of the place, from the rotunda to Statuary Hall, oozes with history and is steeped in tradition. It was humbling to be in a place that I had read so much about in history books and had always dreamed of seeing in person. A decade earlier, I had seen Capitol Hill from the outside; this was my first intimate look, and I was eager to savor every minute. We even got to see a portion of the hearing about changes to the Affordable Care Act. The four of us left D.C knowing that we had shared a truly unique experience. I think it was an eye opener for the guys too. It is quite an undertaking to travel with someone who is disabled. Each of them are phenomenal, active dads with their own children and taking care of my needs during our trip did not seem to faze them one bit.

Your life and mine is comprised of a series of events and people that make up our story. If you take nothing else away from reading this book, remember you are the author of your own book. Its contents are determined by the choices you make and the people you allow to influence it. Be bold in defining who you are and never allow your current difficulties to dictate your future reality. Live beyond your challenges. Seek out your passion and be willing to relentlessly pursue it. Surround yourself with people who fill your life with joy and love you as you are, and when you can, do your part to make a positive impact on the lives of others. These are the lessons I've learned which have guided me through some of the darkest times in my life.

It is my sincerest wish that they provide some small glimmer of light in *your* dark hours. My story is not a special one. Each one of us is presented with our own unique set of challenges, but we are also granted opportunities to overcome them. It has been my experience that success depends on ten percent of our circumstances and ninety percent on how we react to them. You and I have the ability to make choices every day that will determine the course our lives take.

Here's hoping you find the wisdom and courage to make the right ones and find the people that can help you make them. Use the gifts and talents that only you are blessed with to make wherever you are a better place than it was when you arrived. Above all, remember life's most important lesson - be the good in the world!

Acknowledgements

Never again let it be said that it is difficult to write a book. Each one of us has a story to tell. I hope that reading this book has impacted your own, or at least made you think about how you look at it. So many people are responsible for the fact that *my* story is a success. What you hold in your hands is a testament to them, as much as anything else. I first have to start by thanking my mother, Patricia Ham. She was my first teacher and supported me in everything I did. Before she passed I talked about the remote possibility of turning my presentations to students and teachers into a book, and being the personification of humility that she was, she requested that I not dedicate it to her, nor in her words "overstate [my] importance." While I have kept the first part of that agreement, I don't think one *can* overstate the fundamental role she played in my life. I hope that in a certain way this book is a testament to her memory. I owe her a debt of gratitude, greater than she would ever claim, or I will fully comprehend.

Words cannot express my gratitude to Scot Brewer for his encouragement and support, not only throughout this process, but for over half of my life. As the person I love most in the world, our relationship is everything to me. Brew, I thank you for being the brother I always wanted and the mentor that I need; above all for teaching me to be a man who wasn't defined by a physical disability, but by the ability he had to use his strengths to help others. When I was younger, I wanted to be just like you. You are my hero and I hope that in the years since I have lived in a way that makes you proud and achieves that goal. In some measure I want this book to be a tribute to you which inspires teachers who save lives every day, just the way you saved mine. May it make you feel as honored as I am to have benefitted from your example and to have you at my side these many years. I also am immensely grateful to Clarice Francis for being my surrogate mother and allowing me to adopt her and filling a much needed role in my life. I love you, Mom, more than you will ever know or the thoughts contained in this book could ever do justice.

Thanks also to Gene Steinke for reminding me that the message contained within these pages is needed and meaningful to students and teachers alike. You are one of the first men I ever looked up to and one of the only to share my public speaking stage during my time as a student as Troy Junior High. Just as you did when I was 14 years old with my earliest speeches, you inspired me to move forward with this project. Every day I am grateful that my life has been enriched by the presence of someone who is so remarkable. My sincerest thanks and love also go out to Gene's parents, Paula and "Big Gene" Steinke. The gift of your son's life has brought incalculable good to my own. I thank you for raising the man who would become my first hero. Most of all I thank you for taking me into your fold and giving me two perennial examples of truly good people who make my world a better place through their examples.

I also want to thank Chris Karnehm, as the only one of the central characters of the book who I actually let read the manuscript as it evolved. Chris, your expertise was invaluable, reminding me of certain stories and advising me on the content and structure of the text. Most of all, I thank you for showing me a role model of genuine caring and concern for others, while teaching me to find the joy that life has to offer. Thanks to Jen Karnehm for her grammatical advice and early suggestions!

Much appreciation goes to Brad Rohlfs for encouraging me to listen to the audiences who wanted this book to happen. I am grateful to you for always being there to look after me, ever ready to be there with your big heart and willing to see the good in every person and situation. Also, to Brad's family, especially Natalie and Bob and Dianne, for filling my life with so much love and support.

To Mark Evilsizor - thank you for being the best lunch buddy that anyone could ever ask for. Your advice and support has carried me through some of the greatest and most difficult times in my life. Because you showed me the importance of an open mind and heart, I can empathize with the students I speak to in a way that I might not have been able to, but for your influence. The process of writing a book is nothing without a good editor. The dedication of Loren Evilsizor made the idea of this book a reality. Her edits and suggestions added an extra dimension to the book that makes it very special. The fact that Loren played such an instrumental role in the completion of this book means a great deal to me. Not only is she a well-respected educator in the Troy City School District, she is the only female brave enough to sit at our male dominated lunch table at Troy High School. I thank you, Loren, for your support and belief in me over the years, and for being a part of some wonderful memories of a very special time in my life as a student at THS!

Lastly, I would be remiss if I didn't express my unyielding appreciation to the students and teachers who have been a part of all the audiences to whom I have spoken. I know that I was supposed to bring something to them; in truth, however, they gave me so much more. The talks that have led to the book you hold in your hands have enabled me, in an infinitesimal way, to share some of life's most important lessons with you. I only hope that I have made a modicum of the impression on the teachers and young people who have heard me speak and read this book as they have made on me!

42928234R00106

Made in the USA
Middletown, DE
22 April 2019